Table of Contents
WHAT'S FUN ABOUT?

Galveston 9

Brazosport 49

Palacios, Port Lavaca, & Port O' Connor 83

Rockport 105

Port Aransas 143

Corpus Christi 171

South Padre Island 216

Index 274

This book contains descriptions including operating times and admission costs of many of the fun and interesting places in the Houston area. Although a great deal of effort has gone into making this book as up-to-date and accurate as possible, changes constantly occur. Therefore, before visiting a destination, please call to confirm the information provided herein. Neither Into Fun Co. Publications, a division of Into Fun, Inc., the owner, nor the author warrant the accuracy of the information in this book, which includes but is not limited to price changes, addresses, names, hours of operation, management or conditions of the attraction described.

101 Fun Things To Do On THE TEXAS COAST

written by
Karen Foulk

Into Fun Company Publications
A Division of Into Fun, Inc.
Sugar Land, Texas

101 Fun Things To Do On The Texas Coast
by Karen Foulk

Cover and Map Illustrations
by Delton Gerdes
Layout & Formatting
by Karen Foulk & Brocky Brown

Copyright © 1999 Karen Foulk

All rights reserved. No part of this book may be reproduced or transmitted in any form or by any means, electronic, mechanical, photocopying, recording or otherwise, without prior written permission from the publisher.

Library of Congress Catalog Card Number
98-072721

ISBN   0-9652464-2-6

Into Fun Company Publications
A Division of Into Fun, Inc.
P.O. Box 2494
Sugar Land, Texas 77487-2492

Printed & bound in the
United States of America

Into Fun Co. Publications are available for educational, business, and sales promotional use.

Please contact:
Into Fun, Inc.
P.O. Box 2494, Sugar Land, Texas 77479
Phone: 281-980-9745   Fax: 281-494-9745

Dedication

Again, with all my love,
to my husband Don
whom I still have trouble
convincing that I am working.

Michael

Rachel

David

Rebecca

— they don't mind a bit!

Acknowledgments

In appreciation to dear friends and associates, for making this "Into Fun" book possible:

To my husband and children for their support, patience, and kindness.

To Jerrie Hurd, a great sister and a friend.

To Merrill Littlewood, world's greatest accountant; I can't say enough.

To Brocky Brown, for all his dedication on my company's behalf.

To Wendy Nielsen, my "Into Fun" friend, for her time and talents.

To Ken Barrow, for his legal counsel and advice.

To Annette Hruska, who designed my "Into Fun" car.

To Sharon Cooper, always a friend.

I would like to do for the Texas Coast what I have done for the Houston area—let people know it is a "fun" place to go.

Exploring the coast has been an exciting adventure. Now I am saying, "Florida, move over. We've been keeping Texas a secret too long and I'm spreading the word."

I wrote this book with your family in mind. It's handy and fits into the glove compartment of your car or in your purse. It's packed with information, the kind that gives you a pretty good overview of what's really there, yet detailed enough to be used as a reference book. When friends ask me where to eat in Corpus Christi, I pull out the book and tell them in a flash.

The Texas Coast explodes with the kinds of activities that create wonderful family memories. And I believe in wholesome, fun outings and vacations together with our families. Here is the book that will tell you how to do it.

It is also, however, written for anyone wanting an adventure on our coast.

I want you to know that any one of these destinations, such as Galveston Island, Brazosport, Rockport, Port Aransas, Corpus Christi, or South Padre Island would constitute a fantastic vacation in itself. Nevertheless, this book is about all the things you can do on the Texas Coast. I hope you will wear-out your copy of *101 Fun Things to do on the Texas Coast* seeing it all.

Explore on your own and have fun!

Karen Foulk

GALVESTON AREA

Chapter 1
What's Fun About Galveston?

About Galveston	10
Air Tours of Galveston Island	12
American National Observation Area	13
ArtWalks	14
Bolivar Ferry and Port Bolivar Lighthouse	15
Car Museum-David Taylor Classics	16
Galveston Harbour Tours	17
Galveston's Historical Homes	18
Galveston Historic Museum	19
Galveston Historic Seawall	20
Galveston's Beach Parks	21
Galveston Railroad Museum	24
Golfing on Galveston Island	25
Grand Opera House	26
Lone Star Flight Museum	27
Moody Gardens	28
Ocean Star Offshore Energy Center	30
The Great Storm Theater	31
Sport Fishing on Galveston Island	32
The Strand Historic District	34
Tall Ship Elissa & Texas Seaport Museum	35
Watch for these Annual Events	36
What's Kids' Stuff?	37
Where to Eat?	39
Where to Stay?	42
Unique Places to Shop	46

What's Fun About Galveston?

GALVESTON

Galveston—a strong flavor of New Orleans tucked in our own backyard. With its close proximity to Houston, Galveston affords opportunities for a weekend getaway. Fancy restaurants, beautiful historical homes, wonderful resorts, and unique attractions make it one of the country's best-kept secrets.

Rich in history and culture, you'll find the beaches to be only part of the fun. Galveston, known to be hectic and crowded during the holidays, but nonetheless popular all year round, boasts of no off-season. It's rare to find a time that's not good to go.

Surrounding coastal neighbors envy Galveston because she offers so much. And on top of that, everything on Galveston Island lies within a short driving distance.

The pirate, Jean Lafitte, once made Galveston his home. He terrorized the coast and dealt in the slave market. Tales of his buried treasure continue to this day. The location of his treasure remains a mystery.

He was recruited by General Long, husband of Jane Long, "the Mother of Texas," to help fight for Texas' Independence, but he refused to get involved.

At one time, Galveston titled itself the richest city in Texas, the "Wall Street of the Southwest." Those days stay evident when you visit the Strand District or see some of the magnificent old homes.

You'll also find it fascinating to know that Galveston evolved as a major port of entry, second only to Ellis Island for the number of immigrates coming into the U.S.

Galveston holds in memory the worst natural disaster in U.S. history. It would be hard to describe the damage that took place from the Hurricane of 1900. Six thousand people were killed and 1/3 of Galveston was destroyed. Don't miss the tremendous tale of recovery

What's Fun About Galveston?

and success of building the great seawall. The story, retold daily at the Great Storm Theater, impresses everyone.

I'm sure you will enjoy your adventure to this great city on the Texas coast. Have fun!

How many miles from Galveston to
- Austin 209
- Brownsville 399
- Corpus Christi 230
- Dallas 291
- Houston............. 47
- San Antonio 244

What's Fun About Galveston?

AIR TOURS OF GALVESTON ISLAND

2115 Terminal Drive
409-740-4359

See Galveston from a plane

Weather permitting, take a half-hour flight over Galveston's most interesting sights with your pilot as your guide. Popular for vacations and as a gift for birthdays, anniversaries, and Valentines Day. Call a few days in advance for reservations; they are particularly busy on Saturdays throughout the summer.

Hours

Daily by reservation only

Cost

Per Half-hour

Family Tour (3 passengers)	$79
Sunset Tour (3 passengers)	$99

Discovery Flight / Dual Instructional Flight

Half-hour (2 passengers / Katana Plane)	$49
Hour (2 passengers / Katana Plane)	$89

Directions

At the Municipal Airport, next to Moody Gardens.

What's Fun About Galveston?

AMERICAN NATIONAL OBSERVATION AREA

American National Tower
20th and Market Street
409-765-7834

Observation deck on top of the Island's tallest building

Observe from 330 feet high. View Galveston Island from the 20th floor in all directions.

At present, the observation deck is open only to groups of 20 or more with a reservation.

Cost
Per Person $2.50

Directions
Look for the tallest building near the area.

What's Fun About *Galveston?*

ARTWALKS
409-763-2403
An art lover's evening in Galveston

Considered one of the best things Galveston has to offer. One evening every six weeks, galleries throughout the historic downtown area open their doors to extraordinary exhibits and artwork.

Hours
One evening every 6 weeks from 6-10pm

GALLERY ROW

Attend receptions for new works, see national touring exhibits. Most galleries are on Gallery Row, located on Post Office Street, three blocks from the historic Strand. Here are shops and their specialties:

Buchanan Gallery • 2217 Post Office
Original art, paintings and sculptures by contemporary Texas and Southwestern artists.

"E" Street Gallery • 2219 Post Office
Contemporary paintings and metal sculptures.

Galveston Arts Center • 2127 Strand
Features works of intermedics, mid-career artists working in a variety of media.

Innuendo • 2215 Post Office
Regional artists with contemporary and abstract paintings, photography and interpretative works.

What's Fun About Galveston?

BOLIVAR FERRY

900 Ferry Road
Galveston, TX 77553
409-763-2386

Free ferry ride in Galveston

Fun to do with the family or guests. Take the Bolivar Ferry from the east end of Galveston Island to the Bolivar Peninsula and back.

Don't wait to drive aboard if the traffic is heavy. Park in the nearby lot and walk on. From the ferry you will have an excellent view of the harbor. Remember bread for the flock of hungry sea gulls that follow along. Ride takes approximately 18 minutes each way.

Hours

Seven days a week, 24 hours a day

Cost

Free

Directions

Watch for signs for the Bolivar Ferry as you drive around Galveston Island. Take I-45 South to Galveston Island. Follow Broadway (as it becomes Seawall Boulevard) past Stewart Beach. Go left on Highway 87.

PORT BOLIVAR LIGHTHOUSE

After reaching Bolivar Point, drive approximately one mile for a view of the old Bolivar Lighthouse. One of only a few left. Built in 1872.

What's Fun About Galveston?

CAR MUSEUM
DAVID TAYLOR CLASSICS
1918 Mechanic Street
409-765-6590

See classic cars in a historic building

See classic cars immaculately restored and maintained. Representing some of the best of the American automobile industry between the 1920's and the 1960's.

Among this collection are award-winning cars. One, their 1936 Cadillac V-12 Convertible, has won first-place awards five times.

Watch the one-hour video in the museum's theater. Read fascinating 1920's newspaper articles. Many people aren't aware that the building that houses these cars is also a historic landmark.

See such classics as a 1927 Buick Roadster or a 1931 Packard Super Eight 840 Convertible Coupe. Cars are restored from the bare frame or bought with low-mileage and in good condition so they didn't require restoration.

Hours
Daily .... 10am - 5pm

Cost
Adults $5
Senior & Student $4
Children (under 7) .... Free

Directions
Located one block from the Strand District.

What's Fun About Galveston?

GALVESTON HARBOUR TOURS
Pier 22
409-765-1700

Narrative tours of Galveston's Historic Harbor

Choose between a 45-minute narrated tour of Galveston Harbor, a Saturday morning Dolphin Watch or a Saturday Sunset Dinner Cruise aboard the Seagull II, a 50-foot motorized catamaran. You will see the Port of Galveston, Pelican Island and other sites.

Galveston Harbour Tours offers nature tours, wetland excursions and bird watching tours for families, social, civic and school groups of 30 or more. Students K-12 can board a floating laboratory (a tranformed Seagull II) for a state accredited educational tour designed by GHT's Director of Curriculum.

Tour Hours
Memorial Day to Labor Day
(*reservations needed)

Wed. - Fri. - Narrated (45 min)	1, 2, 3pm
Saturday - *Dolphin Watch	8:30am-10am
Narrated (45 min)	12, 1, 2pm
*Sunset Dinner Cruise	6:30-8:30pm
Sunday - Narrated (45 min)	12, 1, 2pm

Cost per person
Narrated Tours (45 min)
..... Adults $6, Seniors & Children $5
Dolphin Watch Tour $10
Sunset Dinner Cruise $40
Educational Tours ...... $6 per student per hour

Directions
Located near the Strand on Pier 22

What's Fun About Galveston?

GALVESTON'S HISTORICAL HOMES

Ashton Villa (1859)

2328 Broadway • 409-762-3933.
Oldest magnificent house on Broadway.
Explore life of wealthy Victorian.
Open Mon.-Sat. 10am - 4pm
Adults $4; Students & Seniors $3.50;
Family $14 (2 adults & children under 8).

Bishop's Palace (1886)

1402 Broadway • 409-762-2475
Ranked among the top 100 homes for architectural significance. Bought in 1923 by the Catholic Church as a residence for the Bishop of Galveston.
Summer: Daily 10am - 5pm; Winter: noon - 4pm
Adult $5; Seniors (55+) & Children(-13) $1.

Moody Mansion (1895)

2618 Broadway • 409-762-7668
The Moodys were very influential in politics and business. A turn-of-the-century Victorian Mansion.
Mon.-Sat. 10am - 4pm; Sun. 1pm - 4:30pm
Adult $6; Child (6-18) $3; Seniors $5.

Powhatau House (1847)

33427 Avenue O • 409-763-0077
Home of pioneer merchant and former
Mayor John Seabrook Sydnor.
Sat. 1am - 3:30pm • Adult $2; Child $1.

Samuel May Williams Home (1839)

3601 Avenue P • 409-762-3937
One of the oldest homes in Galveston. Enjoy the climb up the winding stairs to the widow's walk.
Sat. & Sun. noon - 4pm • Adult $3; Sen. & Child $2.

What's Fun About Galveston?

THE GALVESTON COUNTY HISTORIC MUSEUM

2219 Market Street
409-766-2340

Local artifacts and history

Inside the old City National Bank Building. Note the old bank's architecture and particularly the ceiling. Museum gives you a feel for what turn-of-the-century Galveston was like.

Summer Hours

Mon. - Sat. .... 10am - 5pm
Sunday .... Noon - 5pm

Winter Hours

Mon. - Sat. .... 10am - 4pm
Sunday .... Noon - 4pm

Cost

Adults .... $1 (suggested donation)
Children .... Free

Directions

From Broadway, go left on 23rd.
Follow to Market. Will be on the right.

What's Fun About Galveston?

GALVESTON HISTORIC SEAWALL

The Seawall—avery important part of Galveston, past and present—not only provides protection to the island, but offers a very enjoyable place to spend time.

Galveston's seven-mile-long Seawall rises 17 feet above the ocean front, protecting the island from horrible devastation of hurricanes such as the one that occurred in 1900. This hurricane pounded the island, with tremendous force, killing over six thousand people.

Established in 1904. Extending one-third the length of the island, the Seawall furnishes a 16- to 20-foot base, with a 3- to 5-feet width on top. It contains granite, sandstone, and concrete materials.

At the same time, other structures were raised four to six feet with sand. The Seawall took about ten years to complete and cost $14 million.

The Seawall creates a great place for beachfront running, cycling, walking, rollerblading, and strolling.

SEE-WALL MURAL

Claims to be the world's longest mural. It runs along the Seawall for approximately 2.5 miles (14,760 feet), from 27th to 61st Streets.

Local artists Peter Davis, Jane Young, and Mike Janot created the mural, with the help of some 14,000 volunteers and 8,500 school children.

The scenes depict life on Galveston Island, life in the Gulf, and local birds.

What's Fun About Galveston?

GALVESTON'S BEACH PARKS

Galveston beach parks rank high in popularity on Galveston Island. Some even provide attractions. Thanks to Galveston's beach nourishment project, as much as 150 feet of sand now adds to the width of the beach from 10th to 61st Streets. Public beaches extend within walking distance of many major hotels.

By law, beaches in Galveston remain free of alcohol with a fun family kind-of atmosphere, (except for East Beach-Apfel Park). Beach parks will charge for parking or an entrance fee as in the State Park, plus admission to their attractions.

EAST BEACH - R.A. APFEL PARK
Seawall and Boddecker Drive
409-762-3278

Outdoor pavilion with snack bar, gift shop, showers, volleyball courts, game room, and live musical entertainment in the summer. Big Reef Nature Park is a favorite spot for bird watching.

Hours - Late Feb to Mid-Oct. .... 8am - 6pm
Cost .... Parking $5

GALVESTON COUNTY POCKET PARKS
409-770-5355

Two pocket parks with hot showers, picnic tables, grills, concessions, chair and umbrella rentals.
FM 3005 at 9½ Mile Rd.
FM 3005 at 11 Mile Rd.

Hours .... 9am - 9pm
Cost .... $5 per car

What's Fun About Galveston?

GALVESTON ISLAND STATE PARK
FM 3005

Picnic tables, grills, fresh water, hot showers, camping, and fishing.

Hours .... 8am - 10pm
Entrance Fee per person (13 and older) $3
Overnight Camp Sites
    (Rodeo Range) .... $12.50 - 18.00

PALM BEACH AT MOODY GARDENS
One Hope Boulevard
409-744-PALM

Only place in town with white sandy (man-made) beaches and clear lagoon pools. Like going to the Caribbean. Offers slides and playground equipment for the kids, along with a whirlpool spa. Concession stands. Beach umbrellas for rent. No outside food allowed.

Hours (Summer) .... 10am - 7pm
Cost per person $6

PORETTO BEACH
10th and Seawall Beach

Hours are seasonal
Weekdays .... 10am - 5pm
Weekends .... 9am - 5:30pm
Cost per car $5

What's Fun About Galveston?

STEWART BEACH
6th and Seawall Blvd.
409-765-5023
Offers special attractions.

Hours - Mid-March to Mid-Oct.......... 8am - 6pm
Cost per car................................. $5

Stewart Beach Amaze 'N Galveston
409-765-7020
Giant maze to walk through
Summer (everyday) .... 11am - 11pm
Adults $4, Children (5-12) $3, Re-runs $2

Stewart Beach Water Coaster
409-762-6022
Summer (everyday) .... 10am - dusk
Children (3' or under) w/adult supervision...... Free
Per Person 1/2 hour..................... $6.50
                1 hour....................... $8.50
                2 hour....................... $9.50

Stewart Beach Mini Golf Course
405 Seawall Blvd.
409-762-3935
Summer .... Sun. - Thurs. 10am -10pm
                          Fri. - Sat. 10am - Midnight
Adults 18 holes............................... $4
           36 holes $5.50
Seniors & Children (under 12) 18 holes $3
           36 holes $4.50

What's Fun About Galveston?

GALVESTON RAILROAD MUSEUM

123 25th Street
409-765-5700

Fantastic Collection

Once known as the Galveston Union Depot, the Railroad Museum now houses the largest collection of restored railroad cars in the Southwest. See 47 locomotives, passenger cars, dining cars, freight cars, and cabooses. Families will enjoy climbing aboard and exploring the rail cars. In the Museum, learn about the trains and Galveston's history. See the model display of the Port of Galveston.

Summer Hours

Daily .... 10am - 5pm

Winter Hours

Daily .... 10am - 4pm

Cost

Adults $5
Seniors $4.50
Children (ages 4 - 12) $2.50

Directions

On The Strand. From Broadway, go north on
25th Street and follow to The Strand.
Will be on the left.

What's Fun About Galveston?

GOLFING ON GALVESTON ISLAND

Galveston has two nice golf courses. One is municipal, the other a country club. Check with the hotel where you plan to stay, many have memberships to the Country Club.

GALVESTON COUNTRY CLUB

14228 Stewart Road
409-740-6476 • Fax 409-740-6451
A private 18-hole course with
club house, pro shop and pool.

Daily .... 7am - dark
Closed Mondays

Greens fee for Reciprocal Guests
Tues. - Fri $75
Sat. - Sun. $80
(Carts included)

GALVESTON ISLAND MUNICIPAL

1700 Sydnor Lane
409-744-2366 • Fax 409-744-0272
An 18-hole championship course, Par 72 with a slope rating of 131. Open to the public

Summer .... 7am - dark
Winter .... 8am - dark

Resident's Fees	Non-Resident's Fees
Mon. - Fri. .. $13	Mon. - Fri. $18
Sat. - Sun. .. $15	Sat. - Sun. $25

Carts.................................. $20

What's Fun About Galveston?

GRAND 1884 OPERA HOUSE
2020 Post Office
800-821-1894 • 409-765-1894

100-year-old Opera House

The Grand 1894 Opera House is one of the most elegantly restored opera houses in the country. This was a 12-year, $8 million award-winning restoration project. Note the opulent turn-of-the-century opera boxes, the beautiful stenciling, and the chairs upholstered in royal blue and crimson. The grand staircase has also been restored to its original stateliness.

Since its reopening in 1986, notable entertainers such as Hal Holbrook, Ray Charles, Larry Gatlin, Tommy Tune and Helen Hayes have graced the stage.

The opera house presently seats 1,040 and is known for its extraordinary acoustics. You will enjoy this great old place. Productions range from student performances to Broadway shows and international classics. Call and request their performance schedule.

Tours

Open for self-guided tours
Mon. - Sat. .... 9am - 5pm
Sunday .... Noon - 5pm

Cost

Adults $2
Children (12 & under)..................... Free

Directions
Between 20th and 21st Street.

What's Fun About Galveston?

Texas Aviation Hall of Fame
Home of
LONE STAR FLIGHT MUSEUM
2002 Terminal Drive
409-740-7722

Texas' Newest Aviation Museum

Some of the world's rarest and best restored aircraft. Beautiful facility keeps planes from the elements. Considered one of the best air museums. See a B-17 Flying Fortress, a P-38 Lightning, a Tigercat, a vintage Spartan Executive, and more.

Hours
Daily .... 10am - 5pm

Cost
Adults $6
Seniors $4.50
Children (ages 5-13) $4

Directions
Next to Moody Gardens.

What's Fun About Galveston?

MOODY GARDENS

One Hope Boulevard
800-582-4673 • 409-744-4673
http://www.moodygardens.com

242-acre complex with entertainment

RAINFOREST PYRAMID

The world's largest indoor rainforest is located inside a 10-story glass pyramid with trees, plants, exotic birds, flowers, and butterflies from the African, Asian, and South American rainforests. Wear comfortable, cool clothing, especially in the summer. Opens at 10am.

IMAX THEATER

Experience just how real a movie can be in 3-D films. Starts every hour on the hour and lasts 45 min.

COLONEL PADDLEBOAT

Daily cruises on Offat's Bayou at 12, 2, 4pm. Dinner cruises with dancing on weekends. Cost for cruise is $6 and dinner cruise is $27 per adult, $15 for children (4 to 12). Boarding starts at 7pm; dinner at 8pm.

PALM BEACH

Like going to the Caribbean? Enjoy Texas' only white sand beach and clear blue lagoons. There's a yellow submarine for the kids. Whirlpool spa. Concession stands. Beach umbrellas for rent. No outside food allowed.

Open only in the summer, 10am - 7pm.

What's Fun About Galveston?

DISCOVERY PYRAMID
Second Pyramid features these attractions

LIVING IN THE STARS EXHIBIT

Designed in conjunction with NASA's Johnson Space Center, this exhibit dedicates itself to the future, when man will live in space. Pilot the X-38 Space Station Lifeboat, weigh yourself on different planets and train to dock the space station. Be sure to see this new addition to Moody Gardens. Educational and entertaining.

IMAX RIDEFILM THEATER

Strap yourself in your seat and prepare for a thrilling movie ride. Featuring three 18-seat theaters, each with a 180 degree wraparound screen that allows you to move with the action on the screen. This is the first of its kind in the US.

Hours

Daily .... 10am - 9pm

Cost per person

1 attraction	$6
2 attractions	$11
3 attractions	$16
4 attractions	$20
5 attractions	$25
Children under 3	Free
Seniors & Children (4 - 12)	$1 discount

Directions

Go south on I-45 to Galveston and exit 61st St., right on Stewart St. (turns into Jones), then right.

What's Fun About Galveston?

OCEAN STAR OFFSHORE ENERGY CENTER

Pier 19
409-766-STAR • 713-975-6442

Galveston's new offshore oil rig museum

Climb aboard an offshore rig and experience offshore oil production. Informative and educational. Interesting videos, interactive displays, and models take you to offshore locations worldwide.

Wear comfortable shoes and plan to take your time. Climb a few stairs (elevators available), then walk out on top and get a great view of the harbor. Recommended for the whole family.

Hours

Daily .... 10am - 5pm

Cost

Adults $5
Seniors $4
Students $4
Children 6 and under .... Free

Directions

Near The Stand and the
Fisherman's Wharf Restaurant.
20th and Harborside

What's Fun About Galveston?

THE GREAT STORM THEATER
Pier 21 and Harborside Drive
409-763-8808

Documentary about the devastating hurricane of 1900

Before leaving this area, see the film about the category-five hurricane that hit Galveston in 1900. Thousands died in one of the worst natural disasters in our nation's history.

Hours
Starts every hour on the hour
Sun. - Thur. .... 11am - 6pm
Fri. - Sat. .... 11am - 8pm

Cost
Adults $3.50
Children (ages 7-18) $2.50
Children (under 7) .... Free

Directions
Near The Strand, above Willie G's.
Next to the Harbor House Hotel.

What's Fun About Galveston?

SPORT FISHING ON GALVESTON ISLAND

Fish from one of these three piers, at Sea Wolf Park, or from a charter boat offering deep-sea and bay fishing.

PUBLIC FISHING PIERS

61st Street Fishing Pier
409-744-8365

Winters .... 8am - dark
Summers .... 24 hours

Adults $4;   Children $2;   Seniors $1

Galveston Fishing Pier
90th & Seawall Blvd. • 409-744-2273
A quarter-mile-long pier with a 300 foot "T" head.

Seasonal .... open 24 hours

Adults $6; Children (11 & under) $3;
Seniors (60 and older) $4

Seawolf Park
Pelican Island via Seawolf Parkway
51st Street • 409-744-5738

Fish anywhere at the park from the pier. Offers concessions in the 3-story pavilion. Playground.

Hours .... Sunrise - dusk

(Fishing in park including pier charges)
Adults $2; Children (Under 11) $1; Seniors Free
Parking $5

What's Fun About Galveston?

PUBLIC FISHING ON PARTY BOATS

Galveston Party Boats, Inc.
Pier 19
409-763-5423
Offers 12-hour deep-sea and
4-hour bay and jetty fishing trips.

Deep Sea Trips 7:30am
Bay Fishing (morning departure) 8am
　　　　　　(afternoon departure) .... 1:30 pm

Deep Sea Fishing Costs
Mon. - Fri. Adults $55
Sat. - Sun. Adults $60
　　Children (12 & under) $30

Williams Party Boats
Pier 19
409-762-8808
Offers 12-hour deep-sea fishing trips.

Departure time 7:30am

Cost (Monday - Friday)
　　Adults $50
　　Children (12 & under) $35
Cost (Saturday - Sunday) & Holidays
　　Adults $60
　　Children (12 & under) $40

What's Fun About Galveston?

THE STRAND HISTORIC DISTRICT

Visitor Center
2016 Strand
409-765-7834

Old downtown restored into unique shops

Nationally recognized as a historic landmark district with one of the finest selections of Victorian architecture. See what was Galveston Island's central commercial district in the 19th century.

Features over 100 unique shops. You'll find antique stores, art galleries, restaurants, factory outlets, and more. At Gallery Row (on Pacific Street) you'll discover great antiques and paintings. And don't forget to look for the Peanut Butter Warehouse Antiques (on 20th Street), a one-time peanut butter factory.

Along the port, attractions such as the Great Storm Theater, the Tall Ship Elissa, and the Texas Seaport Museum. Next door is a great place for lunch or dinner—Fisherman's Wharf.

In front of Fisherman's Wharf, at Pier 22, tickets can be purchased for the Galveston Island Harbour Tours. Featuring tour of the Channel, the Harbor, and the Port of Galveston. Ask about their sea ecology and their dolphin watch tours.

The Strand offers a full day or weekend of activities within walking distance of parking the car. The Galveston Island Railroad Museum invites you to park your car with them for the entire day for free, and begin your adventure in their fantastic museum.

The visitor center, with all the information you need, has cassettes for a walking tour, brochures, maps, tickets, and more.

What's Fun About Galveston?

THE TALL SHIP ELISSA and TEXAS SEAPORT MUSEUM

Pier 21
409-763-1877

One of the world's oldest active sailing ships

Explore the decks of the tall ship Elissa. Next door in the Texas Seaport Museum, learn about her rescue from a scrapyard in Greece as you watch the wide-screen presentation ***Elissa: The Longest Voyage.***

Talk to volunteers who maintain this treasure.

Hours

Summer	10am - 5:30pm
Winter	10am - 5pm

Cost

Adults	$5
Seniors 65+	$4
Children (ages.7-18)	$4
Children (6 and under)	Free

Directions

In the Strand Historic District.
Near Strand on Pier 21, Harborside Drive between 21st and 22nd Street.

What's Fun About Galveston?

WATCH FOR THESE ANNUAL EVENTS

Dickens On The Strand
2016 Strand Street
409-765-7834

A Christmas celebration held each year on the first weekend of December, transforming The Strand Historic District into the 19th Century London of Charles Dickens. With its fine collection of restored Victorian architecture, Galveston provides the perfect setting for such an event.

Festive foods, beverages, entertainment, costumes, and glittery parades bring in the Christmas Season. The festival site is generally bordered by Strand and Mechanic Streets and 20th and 25th Street.

Admission is free for anyone coming in 19th-Century costume. Watch for advance discount tickets, $6, at Randall's (a Houston area grocery store chain). General Admission is $8. Children under 12 are free.

Mardi Gras
888-425-4753

Texas-style Mardi Gras. A twelve-day event in February that's becoming bigger every year. More family oriented with city curfews and enforced city ordinances. Enjoy traditional merrymaking with parades, a masked ball, art exhibits, sporting events, and live entertainment. The Strand Entertainment District is roped off. Admission is charged.

What's Fun About Galveston?

WHAT'S KIDS' STUFF?

Along with going to the beach parks in Galveston, I highly recommend taking your kids on the Bolivar Ferry (don't forget the bread for the hungry sea gulls), seeing the Kemp's Ridley Sea Turtle Research Center, the Railroad Museum, the Harbour Tours, and Moody Gardens. These places are already mentioned in the book and you'll need to refer to those pages for information. In this section, I have also included some fun places to go shopping.

GULF STREAM STABLES
8 Mile Road
409-744-1004
Horseback riding on the beach,
even for the beginner.
All rides are guided by professional cowboys.

Open Daily (all year) .... 9am - 4:30pm
Cost .... $15/hr per person

KEMP'S RIDLEY SEA TURTLE RESEARCH CENTER
4700 Avenue U.
409-766-3670 • 409-766-3500

See and learn about the endangered sea turtle at this research facility. More than 10 in your group? Let them know you are coming, call for reservations.

Tues., Thurs., & Sat. 10, 11am, 1, 2pm
Cost: .... Free

What's Fun About Galveston?

KIDS' PLACES TO SHOP

THE DISCOVERY CHANNEL STORE
2326 Strand
409-765-5755
Educational and nature items.

KITES UNLIMITED
2215 Strand (2nd Floor)
Kites, kites, and more kites.

ISLAND SHELLS AND SOUVENIRS
101 Kempner (22nd Street)
Seashells, tee shirts, and the like.

BEST BUDDIES
2211 Strand
Plush toys—stuffed animals and collectible dolls.

What's Fun About Galveston?

WHERE TO EAT?

The Ten Best Restaurants in Galveston

DiBella's Italian Restaurant
1902 31st Street
409-763-9036

Galveston's #1 restaurant. Two brothers own it, using their mother's authentic Italian recipes. Popular with locals and visitors for its delicious food. Dibella's should be high on your list of things to do.

Gaido's
3800 Seawall Blvd.
409-762-9625

The most famous of all restaurants on Galveston Island and best known for their fine seafood. Started by Italian immigrants back in 1911, it is still operated by family members. Be sure to eat here.

Fisherman's Wharf
Pier 22 & Harborside Dr.
409-765-5708

You will find this restaurant as you venture to the portside of Galveston Island. Newly renovated, it offers both indoor and outdoor patio dining along with a great view of the port that includes the restored 1877 Tall Ship Elissa. Try lunching on their restored shrimp boat known as the Ursula M. Norton, originally from Martha's Vineyard in Massachusetts. Excellent specialty dishes along with an excellent view. Offering a fresh seafood market that's willing to ship seafood anywhere.

What's Fun About Galveston?

Fish Tales
2502 Seawall Blvd.
409-762-8545

New to Galveston Island with a fantastic view of the Gulf. The second story features outdoor dining. A great seafood grill with casual dining and great prices. Owned by the same people that own Fisherman's Wharf. Take the family here.

The Original Mexican Café
1401 Market Street
409-762-6001

Authentic Mexican food restaurant. Established over 80 years ago. Original recipes have been handed down to the present. You will want to try this place.

Yamato
2104 61st Street
409-744-2742

Only Japanese restaurant on Island, highly recommended. Serves seafood, sushi, and steaks. Watch as your food is grilled at your table.

Café Michael Burger
8826 Seawall Blvd.
409-740-3639

Very popular and highly recommended place to go. Combines gourmet hamburgers, salads, sandwiches, and German food with great atmosphere and the opportunity for a nice walk outdoors.

What's Fun About Galveston?

Phoenix Bakery and Coffee House
214 Tremont Street
409-763-3764

Great for breakfast or lunch. Plan to relax and enjoy. Strawberry waffles, pastries, sandwiches, desserts, and more.

Landry's Seafood House
310 Seawall Blvd.
409-744-1010

Enjoy outdoor dining and an excellent menu. This is one of the best restaurants on Galveston Island and a family favorite. Be sure to try it.

Nate's Steakhouse & Seafood
1228 Seawall Blvd.
409-763-6283

Very popular with the locals. Also recommended as one of the best restaurants on Galveston Island. Along with seafood, their delicious home cooking includes great beef dishes and chicken fried steak.

What's Fun About Galveston?

WHERE TO STAY?
The Best Places to Stay in Galveston

Best Western Beachfront Inn
5914 Seawall Blvd., Galveston, TX 77551
409-740-1261 • 800-528-1234
A 2-star motel, restaurant within 500 feet, heated pool, cable, and free parking.

Comfort Inn
2300 Seawall Blvd., Galveston, TX 77550
409-762-1166
On the beach, 2 blocks from Fish Tales Restaurant (great seafood), pool, cable, great view of the ocean, kitchenettes in larger suites, and continental breakfast.

EconoLodge
2825 61st Street, Galveston, TX 77551
409-744-7133 • 800-424-4777
Offers pool, cable, 96 units within ½ block of the beach.

Howard Johnson Suites
2525 Jones Dr., Galveston, TX 77551
409-740-1155 • 800-446-4656
Restaurant on premises, heated pool, cable, kitchenettes, and ¼-mile from beach.

What's Fun About Galveston?

La Quinta Galveston

1402 Seawall Blvd., Galveston, TX 77550
409-763-1224 • 800-531-5900
On the beach with heated pool, cable, and
kitchenettes in larger suites.
Denny's Restaurant next door.

Ramada Inn Resort

600 Harborside Dr., Galveston, TX 77550
409-765-5544 • 800-RAMADA
Heated Jacuzzi, cable,
with Chinese restaurant on premises.

Hotel Galvez

2024 Seawall Blvd., Galveton, TX 77550
409-765-7721 • 800-392-4285
Oldest hotel in Galveston; with newly renovated
rooms. Great view of the Gulf. Full service restaurant.
Rooms are small but nice. Outdoor heated pool.

Galveston Island Hilton Resort

5400 Seawall Blvd., Galveston, TX 77551
409-744-5000 • 800-Hiltons.
Newly renovated rooms, each with balcony and
view of the Gulf. Good location, across from the beach.
Tropical outdoor pool. Golf course, 2 miles away.

What's Fun About Galveston?

San Luis Resort and Conference Center
5220 Seawall Blvd.
Galveston, TX 77551
409-744-1500 • 800-445-0090

The nicest place to stay in Galveston. Fifteen stories. All rooms have balconies and face the Gulf. Two full-service restaurants. *The Café* is casual; *the Steakhouse* has great food. Outdoor heated pool, good location across from the beach, 2 tennis courts.

Tremont House
2300 Ships Mechanic Row
Galveston, TX 77550
409-763-0300 • 800-874-2300

One hundred seventeen rooms with the 19th-century charm and the feel of a Bed & Breakfast. Great Service. Stay right in the heart of the Strand District. Heated towel racks and lots of fluffy pillows.

Victorian Bed and Breakfast
511 17th St.
Galveston, TX 77550
409-762-3235

Oldest Bed and Breakfast in Galveston. Victorian mansion on an estate furnished with turn-of-the-century antiques. Three suites with private baths, three shared. Buffet breakfast from 8 to 10am. Butler's pantry full of snacks for guests. Guests can feed the dwarf rabbits in the yard.

What's Fun About Galveston?

RECOMMENDED RV PARKS THAT INCLUDE CAMPING

Dellanera RV Park
10901 San Luis Pass Road
(FM 3005 at 7 Mile Road)
Galveston, TX 77554
409-740-0390 • 409-740-0387

Beachfront RV park including camping, children's play area, picnic sites, grocery store, snack bar, laundry facility, recreation room, chair and beach umbrella rentals.

Galveston Island State Park
14901 FM 3005
Galveston, TX 77554
409-737-1222

Offers picnic tables, grills, fresh water, showers with hot water, fishing, RV and beach camping.

What's Fun About Galveston?

UNIQUE PLACES TO SHOP

Here are four areas to go shopping.

The Strand Historic District

Between Mechanic and Strand Streets, concentrated in a 36-block area, this designated landmark has over a hundred unique shops, with a wide variety of items for sale. You'll find antique stores, art galleries, restaurants, factory outlet stores, an army surplus store, designer clothing stores, gift shops, and much more. My favorite is the "The Old Peanut Butter Warehouse," on 20th Street, a onetime peanut butter factory that now sells antiques, collectibles, and gift items. Park the car and enjoy strolling from store to store.

Gallery Row

On Post Office Street, three blocks from the Strand, this up-and-coming area is known for its art galleries. You'll also find shops with antiques, oriental rugs, jewelry, vintage clothing, china, pottery, and other interesting items.

Pier 21

On Harborside Drive, enjoy portside restaurants and shops.

Along the Seawall

You'll find shops along the beach that carry items like souvenirs, beach balls, tee shirts, seashells, caps, and the like. Fun places to take the kids.

What's Fun About Galveston?

BRAZOSPORT AREA

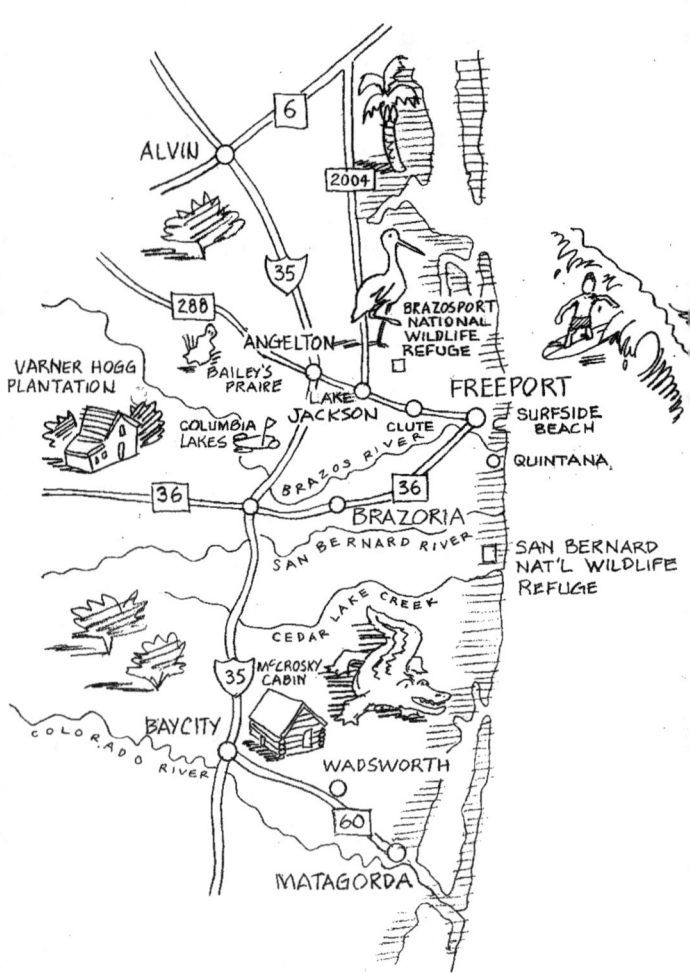

Chapter 2
WHAT'S FUN ABOUT BRAZOSPORT

About Brazosport	50
Abner Jackson Archeological Dig Site	52
Bird Watching Sites	53
Brazoria Center for the Arts & Science	56
Brazoria County Historical Museum	58
Brazoria National Wildlife Refuge	59
Crabbing Sites	61
Deep Sea Diving	62
Dow Chemical Tour Texas Operations Tour	64
Golfing in Brazosport	65
Lake Jackson Historic Museum	66
Port of Freeport	67
San Bernard National Wildlife Refuge	68
Sea Center Texas	69
Sea Shelling in Brazosport	70
Sport Fishing in Brazosport	71
Surfside Historical Museum	72
Texas Nature Adventure	73
Varner-Hogg Plantation State Park	74
Watch for these Annual Events	75
What's Kids' Stuff?	76
Where to Eat?	77
Where to Stay?	79
Unique Places to Shop	81

What's Fun About  *Brazosport?*

BRAZOSPORT

Brazosport—overwhelming in fun family activities, big on southern hospitality, home-style cooking, and comfort.

Mention Brazosport and few people know what you're talking about. This area along the upper Texas coast is a well-kept secret to most Texans. But the fact that it isn't usually thought of as a tourist destination adds to its charm and excitement. Detour here and enjoy the difference.

Leave the commercial fast food chains, resort hotels, nightclubs, and fancy attractions behind. Instead, enjoy these friendly relaxing communities rich in history and nature.

Brazosport offers a family retreat not for the drinking crowds or spring-breakers. Beaches here are so clean, they win awards. Wonderful museums and sites are free to the public or charge nominal fees. For instance, Brazosport is home to the largest exhibit of seashells in the southern United States. See it for free.

Now, what do we mean by Brazosport? A multicity community in southeast Texas, located at the mouths of the Brazos and San Bernard Rivers. The area includes nine cities: Brazoria, Clute, Freeport, Jones Creek, Lake Jackson, Oyster Creek, Quintana Beach, Richwood, and Surfside Beach.

Unlike anywhere else on the Texas Coast, Brazosport features its own distinctive charm. Good food and great places to stay combine with history and nature to make Brazosport a discovery you and your family will never forget.

What's Fun About Brazosport?

Spanish explorer Cabeza de Vaca shipwrecked here in 1528, Stephen F. Austin's original Texas Colony called this area home in 1821. The Battle of Velasco took place near Freeport on June 26, 1832. And this is where the first capital of the Republic of Texas was located.

Today Brazosport is home to the Dow Chemical Company, one of the largest chemical production plants in the world. It plays an important part in building up these communities.

If you love the great outdoors, take the family golfing, crabbing, fishing, shelling, diving, and bird watching.

Best of all—have a great time and I hope to see you around Brazosport!

How many miles from Brazosport to
- Austin 191
- Brownsville 324
- Corpus Christi 171
- Dallas 302
- Houston.............. 61
- San Antonio 225

What's Fun About  *Brazosport?*

ABNER JACKSON ARCHEOLOGICAL DIG SITE

Very Interesting Historical Site

Abner Jackson, a Virginian who came west to seek his fortune, not only built a sugar cane plantation back in the 1840's he left behind his story, one that gets told a little at a time as the earth is stripped away.

Visit this old plantation and see what it was like over 150 years ago. The site is open to the public once a month for guided tours.

Students from Brazosport College and the University of Houston in Clear Lake are digging the ruins of eight different buildings. On the tour, you'll visit the site of the old 12-room mansion, the sugar cane mill, and what remains of a smokestack. These buildings were destroyed in the Hurricane of 1900, which preserved them under earth and debris.

Artifacts are displayed in the new Lake Jackson Historical Museum; others are at the Brazoria County Museum.

Hours
Open for guided tours the first Saturday of every month from 10am to sundown.

Cost
Free

Directions
On the banks of Lake Jackson, northeast 1 mile on FM 2004 from Texas Highway 332.

What's Fun About  Brazosport?

BIRD WATCHING IN BRAZOSPORT

Some of the best bird watching in the country

Bird watchers are on the increase. Did you know that bird watching is now the fastest-growing form of recreation in the United States? But whether you are an avid or a casual bird watcher, you'll find the Upper Texas Coast to be a bird-lover's haven.

Have you ever been to a "fallout"? Neotropical songbirds, after flying 650 miles from the Yucatan Peninsula across the Gulf of Mexico, finally reach land. Exhausted, they almost collapse into trees growing along the Upper Texas Gulf Coast. This annual migratory event takes place in April and May. Radar allows us to track their flight across the Gulf in anticipation their arrival.

To celebrate the songbirds' return home, Brazosport holds an annual bird festival every April, known as "*Migration Celebration*." For more information, call 800-938-4853.

This area is fortunate to have two national wildlife refuges for migratory birds: the Brazoria and the San Bernard. Both are open to the public and provide excellent opportunities for observing wildlife. Call 409-849-6062 for more information.

On the next few pages are some other places for great birding in the Brazosport area.

What's Fun About  *Brazosport?*

BRAZOS BEND STATE PARK
21901 FM. 762
Needville, TX 77461
409-553-5101 • www.tpwd.state.tx.us

Observation tower and platforms provide an excellent opportunity to observe some 270 different species of birds.

FREEPORT MUNICIPAL PARK
409-233-4436

See native birds such as the great-tailed grackle and migrant passerines in the spring and fall. Excellent for warblers, orioles, vireos, and tanagers in the spring.

HANSON RIVERSIDE COUNTY PARK
Brazoria County Parks Department
409-848-0674

Native woodland birds and migrating birds that come through in the spring and the fall. Best time: winter. Located on Highway 35, on the San Bernard River.

LAKE JACKSON WILDERNESS PARK
Lake Jackson Parks & Recreation Department
409-297-4533

Native woodland birds. Migrating birds in spring and fall. Best time: winter.

What's Fun About Brazosport?

POINT WILDLIFE MANAGEMENT RECREATION AREA
Texas Parks and Wildlife Department
409-244-7634
In Bay City. Home to a variety of migrating birds.

QUINTANA ISLAND BIRD SANCTUARY
Quintana Town Hall
409-233-0848
Free to the public. See migratory songbirds, seabirds, and shorebirds.

SAN LUIS PASS COUNTY PARK
Brazoria County Parks Department
409-848-0674
See white pelicans and shorebirds.

VARNER-HOGG STATE HISTORICAL PARK
409-345-4656
Birds native to the woodland area.
Best time to observe migrating birds: winter.

What's Fun About  *Brazosport?*

BRAZOSPORT CENTER FOR THE ARTS AND SCIENCES

400 College Drive
Lake Jackson, TX 77566
409-265-7661

Offers cultural enrichment to the Texas coastal

This 45,000 square-foot complex, owned and operated by the Brazosport Fine Arts Council, promotes the arts and the sciences. You will be amazed at their activities. Most are reasonably priced or free to the public.

ART LEAGUE

With an art gallery, gift shop, and studio, the Art League meets the needs of practically any art lover. They provide art classes for children and adults, "Meet the Artist" receptions, art demonstrations, and a place to purchase quality art pieces. Be sure to see their visiting art exhibits and their gift shop.

Tues. - Sat.	10am - 5pm
Sunday	2pm - 5pm
Cost	Free

CENTER STAGE

Offers theatrical productions and acting classes for children and adults, has its own children's company for grades 1-8. Call for more information and their schedule. Ask to be on their mailing list.

What's Fun About  *Brazosport?*

MUSEUM OF NATURAL SCIENCE

Hosts over 12,000 visitors a year. This museum is small, but has a lot to offer. Free to the public, it is a fun activity for the whole family. A must-see.

See the largest collection of seashells on exhibit in the southern United States. Excellent displays on Gulf Coast wildlife and early history, fresh and salt water aquariums, fossils, dinosaurs, geodes, rocks, minerals, birds, and butterflies.

Great little gift shop with books, posters, shells, minerals, jewelry, marine items, and more. Here you can purchase the Lightning Whelk – "Seashell of the State of Texas."

Museum Hours
Tues. - Sat. .... 10am - 5pm
Sunday. .... 2pm - 5pm
Cost .... Free

NATURE CENTER AND PLANETARIUM

Features a planetarium with a 30-foot dome that seats 72. Presenting a variety of shows throughout the year. The Nature Center Volunteers maintain a beautiful self-guided nature trail outside the complex along Oyster Creek.

SYMPHONY ORCHESTRA

Presents six concerts a year, including a family Christmas concert.

Directions

From Highway 288, turn east on Oyster Creek Dr. and follow as it becomes College Dr. Will be on the left.

What's Fun About  *Brazosport?*

BRAZORIA COUNTY HISTORICAL MUSEUM

100 E. Cedar St., Courthouse Square
Angelton, TX 77515
409-864-1208

County Museum about "Where Texas Began"

Housed in the old 1897 Brazoria County Courthouse, this museum takes you back to the 1900's. Exhibits include unusual artifacts, rare books, and documents, letters from early colonists, and even an oil painting of Stephen F. Austin.

Winner of two awards for the Austin Colony Exhibit depicting the origins of Anglo Texas. This history of how Stephen F. Austin's first 300 settlers arrived at the mouth of the Brazos River and grew in influence until Texas reached independence, is explained in 68 panels covering over 2,400 square feet. Also available is the Adriance Research Library with historical books, documents, and photographs.

Hours

Museum exhibits closed on Monday

Tues. – Fri	9am - 5pm
Saturday	9am - 3pm
Sunday	1pm - 4pm

Cost

Free (Suggested donation $3)

Directions

From Lake Jackson travel north on Highway 288, go right (east) on Highway 35, then left on Velasco Street. Two lights down, go right on Cedar. Easy to see.

What's Fun About  *Brazosport?*

BRAZORIA NATIONAL WILDLIFE REFUGE

Brazoria National Wildlife Refuge Complex
1212 N. Velasco, Suite #200
Angleton, TX 77515
409-849-6062

A great place for observing wildlife and other recreational activities

A refuge is government-owned land set aside to protect wildlife habitats. The Brazoria National Wildlife Refuge was established in 1966 to preserve wintering grounds for migratory waterfowl and other species of birds. It is 43,388 acres, the largest refuge on the upper Texas coast.

Why would anyone want to visit coastal salt marshes? To see the birds, lots of birds. So many birds that the Audubon Society's Annual Christmas Bird Count in mid-December sights more species here than anywhere else in the nation.

Geese, ducks, songbirds, and shorebirds make the Brazoria Refuge their home sometime during the year. The best time for bird watching is early morning or late evening, whether you want to see the winter waterfowl that migration here, the songbirds, or shoreline birds in the spring and fall.

Visitors come to see alligators, river otters, nutria, coyotes, whitetail deer, feral hogs, raccoons, and maybe even a bobcat. Be sure to drive the auto tour. It is possible to see some amazing wildlife from your car. The dense brush and wild vines make the gravel roads an easier means of travel for the animals, too.

What's Fun About Brazosport?

This is also a great place for photography, hiking, fishing, waterfowl hunting, crabbing, and kayaking.

Here are handy things to remember: Snakes are a part of life at the Refuge. July and August are very hot. Take along a jug of ice water, plenty of bug repellent, binoculars, camera, sunscreen, a hat, and your bird identification book. Restrooms available.

Hours

Open the first full weekend throughout the year and the third weekend of each month, November through May. And intermittently during the week from 8am – 5pm.

Cost
Free

Directions

From the intersection of State Highway 35 and FM 523 (at the Palms Shopping Center) in Angleton, take FM 523 for 4 miles to Highway 2004 and continue another 5.5 miles to County Road 227. Turn left and go 1.7 miles to the entrance gate on your right.

What's Fun About  *Brazosport?*

CRABBING SITES
Crabbing can be lots of fun

Crabbing doesn't require much equipment, expertise, or even a license. All you need is 10 feet of fishing line, a net on a pole, a few chicken necks, a cooler, a towel, and some ice. Governing regulations are few; the daily limit is 300 and each crab must be 5 inches across the body. Females with eggs are illegal to catch. You can tell which females have eggs by the red mass attached to it undershell.

Tie a chicken neck to one end of the fishing line. Drop the line into calm water around a pier or jetty and let the bait sink to the bottom. Wait for a definite tug on the line, then (slowly) pull the bait up until the crab is almost to the surface. Scoop the crab up with the net and put it in an ice chest. Crabs won't live long immersed in water, so simply cover them with a wet towel and then a light layer of ice. Crabs will live longer if they're kept cool.

Cooking is easy; drop the live crabs into boiling water and wait for them to turn bright red. Make sure they are still alive before cooking them. Here's where to go crabbing:

Take Highway 332 toward Surfside Beach. Approximately three miles past Clute's city limits, there is a storm levee built to protect the area from extreme high tides due to hurricanes. From the levee to Bluewater Highway, on either side of the street, is an area that's a haven for crabs.

Swan Lake is another crab haven. Take Bluewater Highway east to the crabbing pier. It will be across the street from Stahlman Park.

What's Fun About Brazosport?

DEEP SEA DIVING
Texas Gulf Coast offers some of the best deep-sea diving in the world

Discovered at the turn of the century, these coral reefs, known as the Flower Gardens, are the northernmost coral reefs on the North American shelf. The Gardens' two sections, the East and West banks, provide some of the most scenic diving in the world.

Located 105 miles off the coast of Freeport, these coral reefs are home to a wide variety of sponges, algae, and tropical fish and are preserved as a national marine sanctuary.

Only 70 miles away, Stetson Banks looks very much like what you would find in the Caribbean. Here, reefs fifty feet down in crystal-clear water can be seen from the boat and are considered by some to be even better than the Flower Gardens.

The diving season ranges from April through October. In February, many divers book trips because hammerhead sharks are present then.

Listed below are several resources for exploring the Texas Gulf Coast underwater. Scuba trips to the 350-acre Flower Garden National Marine Sanctuary can be chartered out of Freeport. Not all charters go to the reefs; some offer one-day diving trips to old sunken ships.

Most boats leave in the evening for a 3 to 4 hour trip to the reefs, leaving a full day for diving. Charters will customize their trips, which can include spear fishing near oil rigs and sunken debris for grouper and red snapper.

What's Fun About  *Brazosport?*

For the Good Times II
PO Box 738
Manvel, TX 77578
281-489-0797
Dives to sunken ships and oil rigs
about 40 miles off shore.

Hydro Sport Scuba (Dive Shop)
120 Highway 332 W.
Lake Jackson, TX 77566
409-285-0600

Mon. – Fri.	10am - 9pm
Sat.	10am - 10pm
Sun.	1pm - 6pm

Organizes dives with local charters.

Princess
1203 North Avenue J.
Freeport, TX 77541
409-942-4042

Dives to reefs and the sunken ships. Trips to the sunken ships are for one day and are booked for six people.

Sea Searchers II
900 W. 2nd Street
Freeport, TX 77541
409-230-0333 • 800-396-3483

Offers one-, two-, and three-day diving trips to the Flower Gardens, Stetson Banks, and sunken ships, include meals and unlimited air. Boat sleeps sixteen people plus two dive masters and a crew of five. Can be booked through local dive shops. Will customize trips.

What's Fun About  *Brazosport?*

DOW CHEMICAL TEXAS OPERATIONS TOUR

Tour the world's largest chemical processing complex

A. P. Beutel Building
2301 Brazosport
Freeport, TX 77541
409-238-2011

In 1940, Willard Dow purchased 823 acres and started what is known as the Dow Chemical Texas Operations. It is the world's largest chemical processing complex and offers a 90-minute bus tour every Wednesday afternoon.

Black skimmers, migratory birds, nest each year in one of the plant's parking lots. Learn how this huge chemical company cares for these birds and our environment.

Wednesdays............................. 2pm
Cost .... Free

Directions

Take 288 South through Lake Jackson. Highway 288 South becomes 332. Continue on 332 for approximately 12 miles to the A. P. Beutel Building, a white brick building with green trim, on the right. Turn right and then left into the parking lot or park across the street. Meet in the lobby.

What's Fun About  *Brazosport?*

GOLFING IN BRAZOSPORT

Two public golf courses in the Brazosport area.

Columbia Lakes Resort and Conference Center

188 Freeman Blvd.
West Columbia, TX 77486
409-345-5455

Open daily to the public with pro shop. On Hwy. 35 between Angleton and West Columbia.

Greens Fees (including carts)
Mon. - Thurs. $50
Weekends and holidays $65

Freeport Municipal Golf Course

830 Slaughter Road,
Freeport, TX 77541
409-233-8311

18-hole course, open to the public from dawn to dusk. Offers a driving range, golf supplies, lessons, and club rentals.

Greens Fees
Mon. - Fri. $10
Sat. Sun. and holidays.................... $13
Carts $17.24

What's Fun About Brazosport?

LAKE JACKSON HISTORIC MUSEUM

249 Circle Way
Lake Jackson, TX 77566
409-297-1570

New museum will excite any history buff

This beautiful new facility houses Lake Jackson's history in an exciting new way. Their prize exhibit, the Windecker airplane, catches your attention as you walk through the door. This all-plastic aircraft was the precursor of the stealth bomber and was designed by a local dentist, Dr. Leo Windecker. Although there are many models of this aircraft on display throughout the United States, including at the Smithsonian, the Lake Jackson Historical Museum is proud to have the original.

The whole family will enjoy treasured artifacts unearthed at the Abner Jackson Plantation site.

The museum wouldn't be complete without a section on the Dow Chemical Company, one of the world's largest chemical complexes. Dow Chemical has had a tremendous influence on the area's prosperity and has an interesting story to tell.

Hours—Tues.-Sat. 10am-4pm, Sun. 1-5pm, Closed Mondays.

Costs—Adults $3, Seniors $2.50, Children (ages 8-18) $1, Groups of 20+ $2, Members & Children under 8 free.

Directions—Take 332 into Lake Jackson and turn east in front of the Compass Bank Building on This Way Street. Then go right on Circle Way Street. Will be down the street block.

What's Fun About  *Brazosport?*

PORT OF FREEPORT

1001 Pine Street
Freeport, TX 77542
409-233-2667

Free tour of the Port—home to companies like Dole Fruit and Chiquita Bananas

Did you know that 50% of the bananas consumed in the United States come through the Port of Freeport? This port is open for public tours in both English and Spanish. Call the port for further information.

It is amazing what goes on at a modern port that moves over a million tons of cargo each year. This facility is a major deep-water port with a state-of-the-art container system, a revolutionary method for transporting cargo from ships to trains to trucks.

The Port, with its 60-foot turning basin, is the chief staging site for semi-submersible and tension-leg offshore platforms, huge floating islands which produce crude oil from deep water fields.

The Port also exports large quantities of Texas rice. Rice brokers from all over the world come here to buy rice. See huge grain elevators which auger rice into gigantic hulls of ships tightly secured to the docks.

Dow Chemical and other chemical companies in Brazosport are independent of the Port of Freeport's service, but use some of its 8000 acres in their own shipping operations.

Directions

Take Hwy 332 south as it becomes Business 288, Brazosport Blvd, and then Hwy 36. You will come to a "T" in the road, go left on Pine St.

What's Fun About Brazosport?

SAN BERNARD NATIONAL WILDLIFE REFUGE

1212 N. Velasco #200
409-849-6062

Protected habitat for migratory waterfowl

This refuge is smaller than the Brazoria Wildlife Refuge, which is also part of this large complex. Created to preserve the ancestral wintering grounds for the lesser snow geese, this refuge is also the first land sighted by many songbirds crossing the Gulf from the Yucatan Peninsula in April and May. Many visitors come in anticipation of their arrival.

See many of these birds in great concentration as you enjoy a three-mile, self-guided auto tour around Moccasin Pond or hike one their many trails.

Visitors are welcome at their headquarters, or field house. Here you will find restrooms, brochures, drinking fountains, and friendly conversation.

Hours . . . . Open during daylight hours
Cost . . . . Free

Directions

From the intersection of Highway 288 and State Highway 35, at the west edge of Angleton, travel 7 miles on 288 south to FM 2004 in Lake Jackson. Turn right on FM 2004 and travel 7 miles until it ends at the intersection of Highway 36 and FM 2611. Take FM 2611 south 4 miles to FM 2918 and go left. Go 1 mile to County Road 306. Turn right and go 1 mile to the San Bernard headquarters on the left.

What's Fun About  *Brazosport?*

SEA CENTER TEXAS

300 Medical Drive, Lake Jackson, TX 77566
409-292-0100 • 800-792-1112

The world's largest red drum production facility

Opened March 1996, this state-of-the-art facility is the world's largest red drum production facility, capable of producing 20 million fingerlings a year. This $13 million project is a joint adventure of the Dow Chemical Company, Texas Operations, the Texas Parks and Wildlife Department, and the Gulf Coastal Conservation Association.

A popular family and school group destination, with over 4,000 visitors a week. For guided group tours and hatchery tours, call well in advance for reservations. The facility is closed on Mondays.

Features a "touch tank," two 2500-gallon aquariums, two 5000-gallon aquariums, and a 52,000-gallon aquarium. The exhibits explain marine life in Texas' beaches, bays, jetties, and artificial reefs, and out in the Gulf of Mexico. Meet the mascot "Gordon," a 300-pound grouper.

A half-acre youth fishing pond teaches children saltwater fishing. The pond is stocked with drum, seatrout, sheepshead, and croaker. Future exhibits will include an interpretive outdoor wetlands trail.

```
Tues. - Fri. .......................... 9am - 4pm
Saturday ........................... 10am - 5pm
Sunday.............................. 1pm - 4pm

Cost ................................... Free
```

Directions: At the end of Plantation St., west of Highway 332.

What's Fun About  *Brazosport?*

SEA SHELLING IN BRAZOSPORT

Shelling's a fun activity in Brazosport

Shelling is a popular thing to do in Brazosport. For best results, go early in the morning before people are out and about.

Best times to go shelling are after a big storm and when the tide is extremely low. After a storm, shells may be plentiful on a particular beach, depending on the wind and water currents. Shelling is good around the bays during low tide.

The mouth of the Brazos River, along the Ship Channel, Galveston West Bay, Christmas Bay, San Luis Pass, Bryan Beach, Quintana Beach, and Surfside Beach are good places to go shelling.

There are over 600 species of seashells found on the Texas Coast. Most popular is the Busycon Perversum Pulleyi, commonly known as the Lightning Whelk. It was named Texas State Shell, April 22, 1987, and is found only of the west coast of the Gulf of Mexico.

Bring your shells to the Brazosport Museum of Natural Science, on 400 College Street, and they will identify them for you. The museum has a great shell collection and sells seashell identification books.

What's Fun About  *Brazosport?*

SPORT FISHING IN BRAZOSPORT

FISHING PIERS

San Luis Pass Fishing Pier
Blue Water Highway • 409-233-6902
Lighted, open daily, 24 hours with facilities.

Quintana County Park Fishing Pier
Free pier, no lights, located on Quintana Beach. Take Highway 288 South to FM 1495 going south. Go 2 miles and turn east on County Road 723. Follow to the park.

CHARTER SERVICES

Action Charters (Deep-sea) • 409-265-0999

Bravo Party Boats (Deep-sea) • 409-233-3610

Capt. Elliott's (Deep-sea) • 409-233-1811

Dave Kveton, El Pescador Lodge (Bay Guide)
409-297-9768

David's Charters (Deep-sea) • 409-297-4410

Davis Charters (Deep-sea) • 409-233-5027

Easy Going Charters (Deep-sea)
409-233-2947 • 800-293-2947

Johnston's Sportfishing (Deep-sea)
409-233-8513

Texas Sport Fishing & Yacht Sales (Deep-sea)
409-233-5249

What's Fun About  *Brazosport?*

SURFSIDE HISTORICAL MUSEUM OLD FORT VELASCO

Surfside Beach City Hall
409-233-1531

Museum of local history

Located on the second floor, in the Old Coast Guard Station—now known as City Hall, is a very small museum with a replica of Fort Velasco. The building sits close to where Fort Velasco once stood, at the mouth of the Brazos River. Learn about the battle that took place and see clothing, artifacts from an archeological dig, seashells, and old ship pieces. The museum is open to the public, but you may need to turn on the lights before going upstairs.

Hours

Mon. - Fri. . . . . 8am - 5pm

Cost

Free

Directions

Cross the Causeway and go left on Fort Velasco Drive to Parkway Road and turn right.

What's Fun About  *Brazosport?*

TEXAS NATURE ADVENTURE

P.O. Box 767
Lake Jackson, TX 77566
409-964-4100
800-268-7289

Nature and Birding Tours

Explore the abundance of wildlife on the Gulf Coast—in the marshes, rivers, and bays—on a 24-foot "Carolina Skiff" or venture to "hot" birding spots at wildlife refuges in a 15-passenger van.

Tours can be customized and feature canoeing in the marshes, history, out-in-nature art, and birding classes. Ask about the 2-1/2 day tour that includes birding on High Island and the Bolivar Peninsula, boating to remote tidal marshes, visiting Sea Center Texas, and exploring the San Bernard Wildlife Refuge.

Hours

Call for tour arrangements and schedules.

Cost (per person)

2-Hour Boat Tours	$20
1/2 Day Van Tours	$30
Full Day Van Tours	$50

Directions

Meeting locations are arranged for each tour.

What's Fun About  *Brazosport?*

VARNER-HOGG PLANTATION STATE HISTORICAL PARK

P.O. Box 696
West Columbia, TX 77486
409-345-4656

1824 Mexican land grant issued to Martin Varner, one of Stephen F. Austin's "Old Three Hundred"

Visit this 65-acre historical park along Varner Creek about 50 miles south of Houston in Brazoria County, originally the site of James Martin Varner's sugar cane plantation.

Several others owned the plantation before Texas Governor James Hogg bought it in 1901. When he died in 1906, he left the plantation to his four children. Will, Ima, Mike, and Tom remodeled the house as you see it today.

Booklets for self-guided tours of the park cost $1. Every Christmas the plantation hosts "Christmas in the Park." Call for more details.

Tour Hours for the Plantation House

(Closed Monday and Tuesday)

Wed. – Sat.	9am – 11am
Wed. – Sat.	1pm – 4pm
Sun.	1pm – 4pm

Tour Costs of the Plantation House

Adults	$4
Children (ages 6 – 12)	$2
Children (under 6)	Free

Directions

Two miles north of W. Columbia on FM 2852.

What's Fun About  *Brazosport?*

WATCH FOR THESE ANNUAL EVENTS

Migration Celebration
888-477-2505
800-938-4853

An annual celebration held in the Spring for the beautiful neo-tropical songbirds that fly into the Brazosport area across the Gulf of Mexico on their migration north. Over 300 species of birds are native or migratory to this area. Features birding tours, field trips, speakers, a trade show, and more. Be on the mailing list for this event.

The Great Mosquito Festival
Clute Municipal Park
409-265-8392
800-371-2971

See "Willie Manchew"—the world's largest mosquito—reign at this three-day, nationally recognized festival, which uses the mosquito as an excuse to have fun. The fun includes food booths, a carnival, games, contests, music, arts, crafts, street dances, cook-offs, and more. Folks from around the state and the country attend this affair. Great for the family. Held the last Thursday, Friday, and Saturday in July. Admission charged.

What's Fun About  *Brazosport?*

WHAT'S KIDS' STUFF?

Brazosport is a family-oriented community. Be sure to take the kids to Sea Center Texas and during the spring, on the auto tour of the refuges. The Museum of Natural Science has a Kids' Corner with hand-on exhibits, the Planetarium has children's shows, and the Varner-Hogg Planation has a nice picnic area.

Places mentioned for crabbing, shelling, and fishing will be lots of fun. While on the beach, eat at the Purple Cow—hamburgers for lunch. Beach houses on Surfside Beach are the most affordable—kids will enjoy staying right on the beach. Three more places I would like to tell you about are:

Surfside Waterslides
139 Howard Drive, Surfside Beach
409-233-8572

Offers two slides for kids 36 inches or taller and at least 3 years of age. Open summer months, starting weekends in May and costs $3 for each half hour. Located 1 mile to the right of the causeway.

Train Museum
418 Plantation
409-299-0152

See a layout of Brazoria County in 1955, designed at a child's level of vision. Open Saturdays 10am - 3pm and Sunday 1pm - 4pm. Free.

Disc Golf at Clute Municipal Park
409-265-8392

Disc golf combines disc throwing with the game of golf. Stop into the park's office for rules, tips for playing, and where to buy a disc.

What's Fun About Brazosport?

WHERE TO EAT?
The Best Places to Eat in Brazosport

Home-style cooking, fresh seafood dishes, and casual dress make eating out delightful. Get away from the usual restaurant food, hectic crowds, and fast pace.

Potato Patch
1415 W. Hwy 332
Clute TX
409-265-4285

One of the most popular places to eat in the area. Family owned and operated. Known for a unique southern home-style cooking: try their stewed apples, fried green tomatoes, and fried okra. Famous for "throwed rolls"—a waiter throws patrons all-you-can-eat, fresh-baked rolls. A very good place to eat.

Red Snapper Inn
402 Blue Water Hwy
Surfside Beach, TX
409-239-3226

Claims their seafood swam in the Gulf the night before it's served— very fresh. Serves excellent dishes such as Shrimp Fettuccine Alfredo and Chicken Fried Steak. Great décor and atmosphere. One of the best seafood restaurants on the Texas Coast.

What's Fun About Brazosport?

Kitty's Purple Cow
Ocean Ave. at Blue Water Hwy.
Surfside Beach, TX
409-233-9161

A place to lunch while having fun on the beach. Very casual atmosphere. Great hamburgers, sandwiches, chicken fried steaks, and seafood. Get home-style cooking, on the beach. Family oriented.

The Kolache Shop
120 Brazosport Blvd.
Clute, TX
409-265-3352

This family owned bakery serves the best kolaches in Brazosport. Popular for their cream cheese kolaches, cinnamon rolls, and pigs-in-a-blanket. Opens 5 am – Noon, Monday through Friday.

On the River
919 W. Second
Freeport, TX
409-233-1352

Another great Texas Coast seafood restaurant. House favorites include blackened catfish, stuffed shrimp, Cajun grilled shrimp, baked flounder. With great salads, sandwiches, and burgers. Be sure to end with the blackberry or peach cobbler.

What's Fun About Brazosport?

WHERE TO STAY?

The best places to stay in Brazosport

Anchor Bed & Breakfast

Anchor Drive, San Luis Pass, 409-239-3729

Offers two rooms for couples and two larger rooms for families or group gatherings.

Rooms include breakfast and dinner served family style with a light lunch and plenty of snacks. Small pets allowed. Caters to fisherman.

Anchor Motel

1302 Blue Water Highway
Surfside Beach, TX 77541, 409-239-3543

An old, well-run 32 unit motel, that's 100 yards from the beach. Some units have kitchenettes. The motel is a mile from the causeway to the right.

Best Western Motel

915 Hwy. 332, Lake Jackson, TX 77566
409-297-3031 • 800-528-1234

Large swimming pool, cable, remodeled rooms, guest laundry, and free continental breakfast. Children under 17 stay free.

Holiday Inn Express

809 Highway 332, Clute, TX 77531
800-Holiday • 409-265-5252

Complimentary continental breakfast offered daily. Amenities include a hot tub, pool, cable TV, and a complimentary pass to the nearby Gold Gym. Built in 1995. Conveniently located.

La Quinta Inn
1126 Highway 332, Clute, TX 77531
409-265-7461 • 800-531-5900

Located three miles north of Freeport with 136 rooms, a heated pool, cable TV, and complimentary breakfast.

Surfside Motel
330 Coral Court, Surfside Beach, TX 77541
409-233-4585

Offers rooms with or without kitchenettes. This motel is an old, well-known establishment. Having no frills, it is clean, well-run, and a 100 yards from the beach. Located a quarter of a mile to the left as you cross over Surfside Bridge. Caters to families who want to enjoy the beach.

Beach Resort Rentals
409 E. Hwy. 332 Suite #2
Surfside Beach, TX 77541
409-233-4900 • 800-382-9283

Rent a beach house for a fun family vacation. Offers weekly, weekend, or weekday rates at some of the most reasonable prices around on the coast.

RV PARKS AND CAMPING

Quintana Beach County Park
On Quintana Beach, 800-872-7578

Offers an RV Park, camping, picnic area, boardwalks, nature trails, interpretive center, fishing pier, beach, playground, restrooms, and showers.

San Luis Pass County Park
Bluewater Highway, 800-372-7578

Visitor center with a deck over the water, fishing pier, boat ramps, cabins, and playground. Located at the foot of the Galveston Toll Bridge.

What's Fun About  *Brazosport?*

UNIQUE PLACES TO SHOP
Shop for Antiques

If you love antiques, you'll want to shop the antique stores in the Brazoria County communities. The communities of Alvin and Angleton have over 50 antique dealers. Stop by the chamber of commerce or one of the antique stores in town for a map to others in the area. Antique stores can be found in the old downtown districts in Freeport, Brazoria, and West Columbia.

BRAZOS MALL

Features many well-known and unique stores. In Lake Jackson on Highway 288 as it becomes 332.

SPECIALTY SHOPS

Buy the Seashell
917 Seashell Dr., Surfside
409-233-8160

Sea Pals
301 Oyster, Surfside
409-239-2224

Old River Trading Co.
220 W. Park, Freeport
409-233-4669

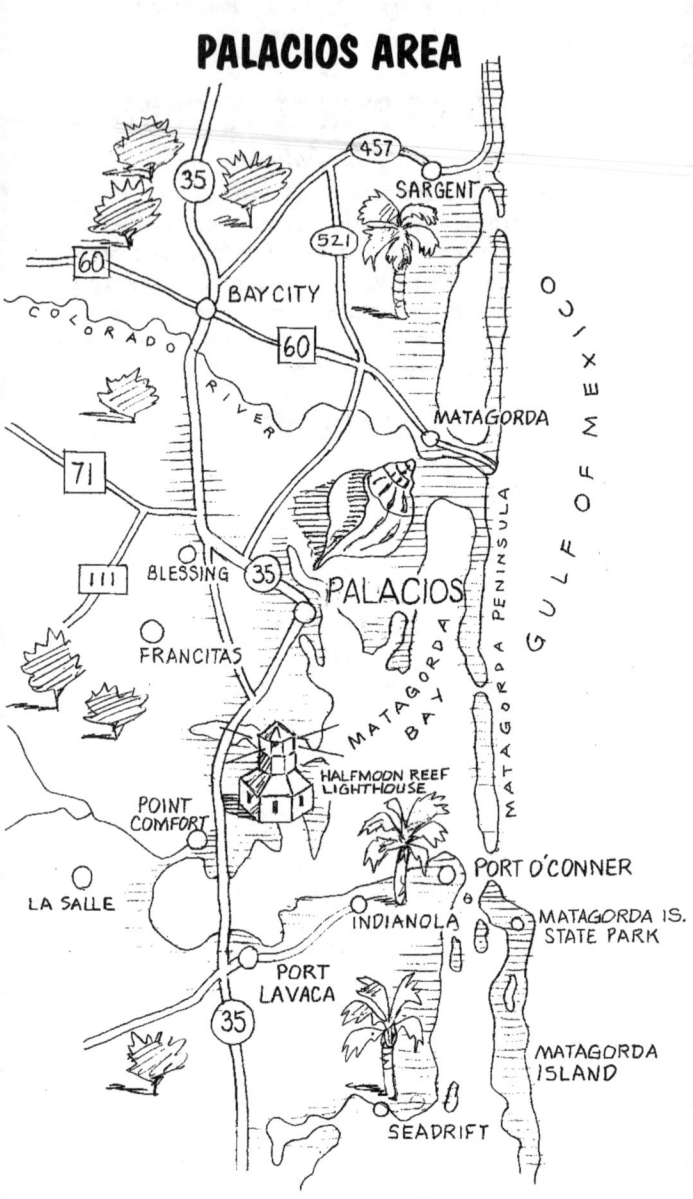

Chapter 3
WHAT'S FUN ABOUT PALACIOS, PORT LAVACA & PORT O'CONNOR?

About Palacios, Port Lavaca, & Port O'Connor	84
Beaches, Sea Shelling, and City Parks	86
Bird Watching Sites	88
Calhoun County Museum	90
Golfing the Coastal Bend Area	91
Matagorda Island State Park	92
Port Lavaca State Fishing Pier	94
Interesting Historical Sites & Markers	95
Sport Fishing the Matagorda Peninsula Area	97
Watch for these Annual Events	99
Where to Eat?	100
Where to Stay?	101

What's Fun About  Palacios?

PALACIOS, PORT LAVACA & PORT O'CONNOR

Palacios, Port Lavaca, and Port O'Connor—land of riches. Rich in history, legends, nature, fishing, birding, boating, camping, shelling, skiing, sailing, and most of all, fun!

It's time to reactivate the fishing poles retired in the garage. You'll find the bays loaded with fish. All types of surf, wade, fly, jetty, shore, and offshore fishing are excellent.

Come with adventure in mind. See roadsides dotted with historic markers. Among the many interesting sites to see, the statue of LaSalle rates the most popular, marking the spot where it's believed he came ashore on Indianola Beach. He's a lone man in the town of Indianola, once the busiest port on the Texas Coast until it was washed away in a hurricane in 1886.

Relax and enjoy the small town life in Palacios. Spend the evening strolling along the lighted seawall; stay in an historic inn or RV Park with a fishing pier and a swimming pool. It is said that Spanish sailors, lost in Matagorda Bay, sailed into Tres Palacios Bay and saw three magnificent palaces with beautiful surroundings. It was only a mirage, yet the weary sailors landed near present day Palacios and christened the spot "Tres Palacios"—the place of three palaces.

The town of Port Lavaca was settled in 1843. The area was already a thriving port, exporting cotton bales, hides, tallow, and cattle. Most of the imported supplies were loaded onto wagon trains for settlements further north and west.

What's Fun About  *Palacios?*

Port Lavaca was fired upon with cannonballs during the Civil War. You can see homes in Port Lavaca that still wear the marks.

Yes! Camels once roamed Texas. In 1856, camels were unloaded in Port Lavaca as part of a plan to help solve the Army's transportation problems. The idea failed. Many of the camels died or were set free.

The town of Alligator Head was later renamed Port O'Connor, after Thomas O'Connor, owner of the original land grant. Catch the ferry in Port O'Connor to Matagorda Island, a remote barrier island with a state park and wildlife refuge.

Make this part of your thrilling adventure on the Texas Coast; but beware, folks seeking genuine family time communing with nature may get a pleasant overdose.

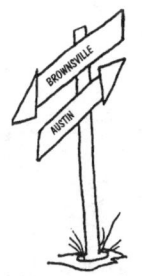

How many miles from Palacious to
- Austin 170
- Brownsville 290
- Corpus Christi 110
- Dallas 352
- El Paso 721
- Galveston 96
- Houston 110
- San Antonio 145

What's Fun About  *Palacios?*

BEACHES, SEA SHELLING, AND CITY PARKS

With all the bays in this area, shelling can be excellent. Best time to go is when the tide is low. Tide is low in the winter months and August.

Lighthouse Beach Park
700 Lighthouse Beach Road
512-552-6097

Port Lavaca's largest park with sandy beaches, fishing pier, boat ramp, nature walkways, camping, picnic tables, children's playground, and swimming pool.

Magnolia Beach Park
Indianola

One of two beaches in Indianola. It was built in 1979, with 15 sheltered picnic tables, barbecue grills, fishing, and a restricted area for swimming.

Indianola Beach Park
Indianola

Two old cemeteries close by. One is by Powderhorn Lake on County Road 112, the other, Old Town Cemetary, is on the ridge. The park has barbecue facilities and blue picnic tables.

Seadrift Bayfront Park
Seadrift
Bayfront picnicking, children's playground, and pavilions.

What's Fun About  *Palacios?*

Bayfront Beach Park
Port Lavaca
512-552-9798

Located next to Nautical Landings Marine, on Commerce and Main Streets, in Port Lavaca. Fort-like playground, covered picnic tables.

Point Comfort Park
Point Comfort

Walking trails, playground, playscape.

Chocolate Bayou Park
Highway 238

Over 40 acres, with fishing ponds, canoeing canals, a picnic pavilion, barbecue facilities, restrooms, and community gardens. Coming will be an amphitheater and boardwalks.

What's Fun About  *Palacios?*

BIRD WATCHING SITES

Calhoun County is a magnet for migratory birds. Listed are some popular birding places. Other known birding sites are the ferry ride to Matagorda Island, the Bayous of the Guadalupe, the Olivia area, and the Port Lavaca State Fishing Pier. For the past six spring migrations, Calhoun County has been number one for the most species of birds sighted in the North American Migration Count.

Formosa Wetlands Walkway and Alcoa Birding Tower
700 Lighthouse Beach

The tidal basin near Lighthouse Beach in Port Lavaca is home for many species such as rails, clippers, roseate spoonbills, herons, night herons, egrets, dowitchers, and dunlins. Climb the Alcoa Bird Tower and observe the wildlife in these marshlands. The walkway is made of 100% recycled plastic milk jugs and has interpretive signs.

Guadalupe Delta Wildlife Management Area

Located 7 miles northeast of Tivoli, this wildlife management area is open to the public year-round and is a great place to see waterfowl and shoreline birds around Buffalo Lake. The area has an observation platform and is a popular place for seeing the wood stork in late summer or early fall.

Indianola Beach, Powderhorn Lake Area, and Magnolia Beach

Around Indianola Beach you can observe curve-billed thrashers, long-billed thrashers, and Bewick's wren. Near the mouth of Powderhorn Lake see roosting

What's Fun About  *Palacios?*

waterbirds and the American oystercatcher. Observe cranes, geese, and other shoreline birds. Magnolia beach is a great place for sandhill cranes, snow geese, and hawks in the wintertime and shoreline birds like the buff-breasted sandpiper, hudsonian godwit, and the wilson's phalarope in the springtime. Take S.H. 316 to Indianola Beach.

Mad Island Marsh Preserve
512-972-2559

Owned and operated by the Nature Conservancy of Texas, Inc., this wildlife preserve has a visitor center and is open for public tours with an on-site staff. Make reservations at least 2 weeks in advance.

Matagorda Island

With over 300 species of bird on the island including 11 species on the endangered list, Matagorda Island is a wonderful place for birding. During the summer months, as many as 37 different species nest there including the white-tailed hawk, black-shouldered kites, Wilson plovers, least terns, wood stocks, and frigates. Popular spring birds are the warblers, buntings, orioles, tanagers, thrushers, black skimmers, American oystercatchers, and white and brown pelicans. Nature tours on the island are offered, contact the park service for more information.

Sun Island

An island six miles from Port O'Connor known as "Bird Island" is a nesting habitat to more than 18 species of birds. The island is protected and observed only by boat. This is the nesting grounds for the brown pelican, snowy egrets, scarlet ibis, roseate spoonbills, reddish egrets, blue herons, oystercatchers, black skimmers, white-faced ibis, some species of gulls and terns.

What's Fun About  *Palacios?*

CALHOUN COUNTY MUSEUM
301 S. Ann St.
Port Lavaca, TX 77979
512-553-4689

History of the Early Days in Calhoun County

The Calhoun County Museum, once housed in the old 1896 county jail, is now next door in the old public library, across the street from the courthouse. It is a museum of Calhoun County's history, with an 8-foot scale model of 1875 Indianola, destroyed by a hurricane that same year and again in 1886, and the lens from the 1852 Matagorda Lighthouse. During the Civil War, Confederate soldiers removed the lens and attempted to destroy the lighthouse. The lens was restored in 1873 and served until 1977, when it was replaced with an electricly powered light. The lens is on loan to the museum from the U.S. Coast Guard.

Hours
Tues. - Thurs. .... 1:30pm - 4:30pm
Saturday .... 10am - 2pm

Cost
Free

Directions
On Ann Street, 2 blocks south of Main.

What's Fun About  *Palacios?*

GOLFING IN COASTAL BEND AREA

Hatch Bend County Club

P.O. Box 141
Port Lavaca, TX 77979
512-552-3037

Public welcome, memberships available.
Swimming pool, tennis courts, club house.
Located 6 miles south of S.H. 87/35, on S.H. 35 going south. Turn right on Meadow Lane (watch for the sign) and go one mile.

Palacios Golf Course

Airport Road, Hwy 35
Palacios, TX 77465
512-972-2666

Open to the public every day from 8 am to 8 pm. A 9-hole course. Green fees are $6 during the week and $8 on weekenks. Carts are $7.1

What's Fun About  *Palacios?*

MATAGORDA ISLAND STATE PARK

P.O. Box 117
Port O'Connor, TX 77982
800-792-1112 Information
512-983-2215 Ferry reservations
512-389-8900 Bunkhouse reservations
www.tpwd.state.tx.us

Camp on a Remote Island and Wildlife Refuge

Matagorda Island, a 56,668-acre barrier island with 38 miles of undeveloped beaches, is a wildlife haven with many endangered species: the brown pelican, the whooping crane, Kemp's Ridley Sea Turtle, and the peregrine falcon. Rich in history, the island was once inhabited by Karankawa Indians and explored by Cabeza de Vaca, Rene Robert Sueir de La Salle, and Jean Lafitte. You'll see the Matagorda Lighthouse built in 1852, old Civil War trenches, and an old abandoned Air Force base.

Located 11 miles from the shore, the island is accessible by boat. The Park offers ferry service from Port O'Connor to the island and a shuttle service to some of the popular beach areas. Mountain bikes are allowed on the ferry and can be used on the dirt roads.

The Matagorda Island State Park, on the northeast end of the island, features shaded picnic tables, showers, fire rings, two bunkhouses furnished with linens and bathrooms, shelling, fishing, hiking, birding, surfing, beach and bayside camping. Camping is primitive. Fresh water or telephones are not available on the island. Swim at your own risk.

 What's Fun About Palacios?

Hours
Ferry operates Thurs., Fri., & Sat.
Departs Port O'Connor 8am, 10am, 3pm
Departs Island 9am, 2pm, 4pm

Cost
Ferry
    Adults $10
    Children (under 12) $5
Bunkhouse/per/night $12
Campsites $4

Directions
On 16th Street and the Intracoastal Waterway, follow the signs.

What's Fun About  *Palacios?*

PORT LAVACA STATE FISHING PIER

202 North Virginia
Port Lavaca, TX 77979
512-552-6097

Popular place to fish

Port Lavaca State Fishing Pier was the old State Highway 35 causeway until it was destroyed in a hurricane in 1961. It is now a 3200-foot lighted pier with restrooms, a snack bar, and fish cleaning facilities.

Nearby, the Port Lavaca City Park offers camping, a boat ramp, and picnic tables.

Hours
Daily .... 24 hours

Cost
Cost per person $2

Directions
As you cross the causeway (on SH 35) coming into Port Lavaca, the fishing pier will be on the left.

What's Fun About Palacios?

INTERESTING HISTORICAL SITES AND MARKERS

Calhoun County is rich in history

Half Moon Reef Lighthouse

2300 State Highway 35, Port Lavaca

The Half Moon Reef Lighthouse, built in 1858 on Half Moon Reef in Matagorda Bay, served mariners coming in and out of Port Lavaca and Indianola. It was damaged in the Civil War but restored in 1868. The lighthouse remained in operation until 1941, when the Japanese bombed Pearl Harbor and the U. S. Coast was blacked out.

In 1942, the lighthouse was severely damaged in a hurricane and was moved to a different location. After several moves, it has been extensively restored and is now located next to the Bauer Community Center in Port Lavaca.

Ranger Cemetery

This is the oldest cemetery in Calhoun County. It became known as Ranger Cemetery after Margaret Plyton Lytle was buried there in 1850. Her husband, Major James Wyatt, "the poet" of the Texas Rangers, was killed in a Comanche Indian raid in Linnville in 1840 and was the first to be buried in this cemetery. It is said that he and his wife returned to the house to get a gold watch. He was killed and his wife was kidnapped but later rescued. Burial plots of pioneers, cholera victims, confederate soldiers, and other interesting people. The cemetery is on Harbor Street in Port Lavaca.

What's Fun About  *Palacios?*

LaSalle's Cross

The Grace Episcopal Church at 213 E. Austin, Port Lavaca, houses the cross LaSalle carried as he landed in Indianola in 1685. Open for the public.

LaSalle Monument

This 22-foot statue of Rene Robert Sueir de La Salle, the French explorer who landed in Indianola in 1685, is practically all that's left of this port city. The statue was placed where LaSalle is believed to have come ashore. Take S.H. 316 to Indianola beach and go south on paved beach road.

Indianola Town Site

Now a ghost town, Indianola was at one time the busiest port on the Texas Coast. Carl Solms-Braunfels and his colony of German immigrants first settled this area in 1844. The town withstood many disasters: the Civil War, yellow fever epidemics, and hurricanes. The hurricane of 1886 washed the town away. It was never rebuilt. The remaining site is considered an important landmark. From the LaSalle Monument, take the unpaved beach road .7 miles; you'll find historical markers where the townsite once stood and a granite boulder marking the site of the old courthouse.

Matagorda Island Lighthouse

The 96-foot lighthouse, on the east end of Matagorda Island, can be seen from Port O'Connor. It was originally built in 1852 and was only 75 feet high. Damaged during the Civil War, it was later reconstructed in its present location. The light was automated in 1956 and then changed to solar power in 1977. The U.S. Coast Guard owns and operates the lighthouse. It is on the National Register of Historic Places.

What's Fun About Palacios?

SPORT FISHING THE MATAGORDA PENINSULA AREA

Known for the best bay fishing on the Texas Coast, Lavaca Bay, Matagorda Bay, Espiritu Santo Bay, San Antonio Bay, and Caranchua Bay have excellent fishing for redfish, shark, trout, whiting, croaker, sheepshead, drum, jack crevalle, Spanish mackerel, and tarpon.

Here some tips for fishing the area: Pass Cavallo is a hot-spot for tarpon; the fishing is excellent on the Matagorda Ship Channel Jetties; East and West Matagorda Bays are best-kept secrets for catching speckled trout and redfish; and surf fishing is wonderful on any beach in Calhoun County.

The Colorado River is a choice fishing spot in the fall when the temperature of the water in the bays drops due to a cold front. The redfish and speckled trout seek the warmer waters of the Colorado River, creating a fisherman's idea of heaven.

Offshore fishing, a short distance out from the Matagorda Ship Channel or from Sargent, is good fishing for snapper, dolphin, kingfish, and ling.

These fishing guides are eager to assist you with a fun day of fishing, either in the bay or offshore. Some offer hunting, bird watching tours, surf fishing, fly fishing, diving, and shuttle service to Matagorda Island. All the guides listed on the next page are members of the Coastal Bend Guides Association.

What's Fun About Palacios?

Capt. John "Red" Childers
P.O. Box 11, Port O'Connor, TX 77982
512-983-2937
Bay, Surf, Duck Hunting, and Matagorda Island

Capt. Robert E. "Bob" Dooley
P.O. Box 532, Port O'Connor, TX 77982
512-983-4230
Bay, Surf, Duck Hunting, Birding,
and Matagorda Island trips

Capt. Ron Elkins
P.O. Box 31, Port O'Connor, TX 77982
Bay, Surf Fishing, and Matagorda Island trips

Capt. Kenneth Griffin
P.O. Box 629, Port O'Connor, TX 77982
512-983-4535
Bay, Night Fishing, and Jetties

Capt. R.H. "Dick" Keitt
P.O. Box 270, Port O' Connor, TX 77982
512-983-4767
Bay, Jetty, Surf, and Offshore Fishing

Capt. Lynn V. Smith
P.O. Box 522, Port O'Connor, TX 77982
512-983-4434
Bay, Surf, Fly Fishing, and Matagorda Island

Capt. Shelby Stocks
15514 Creekhaven, Houston, TX 77084
512-983-4206 • 281-463-7233
Bay, Offshore, Diving Charters and
Matagorda Island trips

What's Fun About Palacios?

WATCH FOR THESE ANNUAL EVENTS

Bay Days (June)

Held in Port Lavaca at the Bayfront Pensinula. The "Best Little Beach Party in Texas," with arts, crafts, children's activities, a carnival, live entertainment, food, jet-ski races, and more. 800-556-Port

Calhoun County Fair (October)

Features a downtown parade, a barbecue and a chili cook-off. The fair includes livestock judging, an auction, and a large carnival. 800-556-Port

Poco Bueno Invitational Offshore Fishing Tournament (July)

Big prize money for this event. Includes catching blue marlin or sailfish. 800-566-Port

"Something's in the Air" (April)

Hot air balloons, kites, and more. Great for families. Features food booths and arts and crafts. 800-611-4567

Palacios Fish Festival (August)

Divisions for everyone, including the kids. Shore fishing allowed. Registration includes a Captain's dinner and more. 800-611-4567

Palacios Fish Fry (October)

After fishing in the Fish Festival in August, return for the fish fry in October. A community fund raising event open to the public. 800-611-4567

What's Fun About  *Palacios?*

WHERE TO EAT?

The Best Places to Eat

These are restaurants with great reputations. Most of these well-known establishments specialize in seafood and home-style cooking.

Barklett's Restaurant
Hwy. 185, Seadrift • 512-785-2441
Opens daily at 11am - 9:30pm. Serves seafood, chicken fried steak, and burgers. Try the seafood platter.

Blackbeard's Restaurants
416 Main St., Palacios • 512-972-2413
Formerly known as Petersen's. Family-oriented, serving seafood, burgers, chicken, pie and more. Try the fried shrimp. Offers children's menu.

Clark's Restaurant & Marina
7th Street and the Intracoastal Waterway
Port O'Connor • 512-983-4388
Popular with locals. Serves seafood, Cajun shrimp, and sandwiches, with gift shop, retail store, boat ramp, and marina. Closed Mon. & Tues.

El Patio Restaurant
548 W. Main, Port Lavaca • 512-552-6316
Authentic Mexican food. Great breakfast menu and with lunch specials Monday-Friday.

Gordons's Restaurant
2615 N. Hwy 35, Port Lavaca • 512-552-1000
Opens daily at 11am -10pm. Serves seafood, steaks, burgers, and has a bakery.

What's Fun About Palacios?

WHERE TO STAY?
The Best Places to Stay

Places listed are well-known Texas historical landmarks. Included are some regular motels, R.V. parks, and campgrounds.

Moonlight Bay Bed & Breakfast
506 South Bay Blvd., Palacios, TX 77465
512-972-2232 • 800-714-1997 ext. 51
Stroll the seawall, a nice weekend retreat.
Serves a hot breakfast.

The Luther Hotel
408 S. Bay Blvd., Palacios, TX 77465
512-972-2312
An historical Texas inn on 5 acres
with view of Palacios Bay.

Hotel Blessing, Coffeeshop & Restaurant
On FM 616, west of SH 35, Blessing, TX
512-588-9579

Eleven miles north of Palacios. Built in 1906, this hotel is a Texas historical landmark that's on the National Register of Historic Places. It has 20 air-conditioned rooms.

Hotel Lafitte Bed and Breakfast
302 E. Bay Avenue, Seadrift, TX
512-785-2319

Built in 1909, this historic landmark faces San Antonio Bay, with a large sun deck, veranda, and rocking chairs. Bonnie and Clyde once spent a night at this hotel. Each room is decorated with Victorian antiques. Offers home-cooked meals with fresh baked bread. No pets or children under 12 allowed.

What's Fun About Palacios?

MOTELS

Days Inn
2100 N. Bypass 35
Port Lavaca, TX 77979
512-552-4511
Room service, cable TV, and guest laundry.

Chaparral Motel
2096 N. Bypass 35
Port Lavaca, TX 77979
512-552-7581
Continenntal breakfast, laundry,
refrigertor & microwave in suites

Executive Inn
2007 N. Bypass 35
Port Lavaca, TX 77979
512-552-1050
New motel, pool, cable, Jacuzzi in suites,
continenntal breakfast, refrigertor & microwave

Port Motel
14th and Commerce Streets
Port O'Connor, TX 77982
512-983-2724
Air-conditioned rooms with kitchenettes and TV.

What's Fun About  Palacios?

RV PARKS AND CAMPGROUNDS

Bayfront R.V. Park
902 First Street
Palacios, TX 77465
512-972-2056
Bay fishing from the bay. RVs only.

Lighthouse Beach & Bird Sanctuary R.V. Park
700 Lighthouse Beach Dr.
Port Lavaca, TX 77979
512-552-5311
City owned and operated with campsites on the waterfront or hill, restrooms, picnic shelters, phone, cable TV, water, and electricity.

Powderhorn R.V. Park
Route 2 Box 187
Port Lavaca, TX 77979
512-552-7481
Camping, showers, restrooms, recreation room, laundry, 5 minutes from the beach. Take SH 316 to the Indianola Beach Parks. Watch for signs

Serendipity Resort
1001 Main Street
Palacios, TX 77465
512-972-5454
800-556-0534
Lots of amenities, marine, camping, pool, beach, fishing pier, bay house for rent.

ROCKPORT AREA

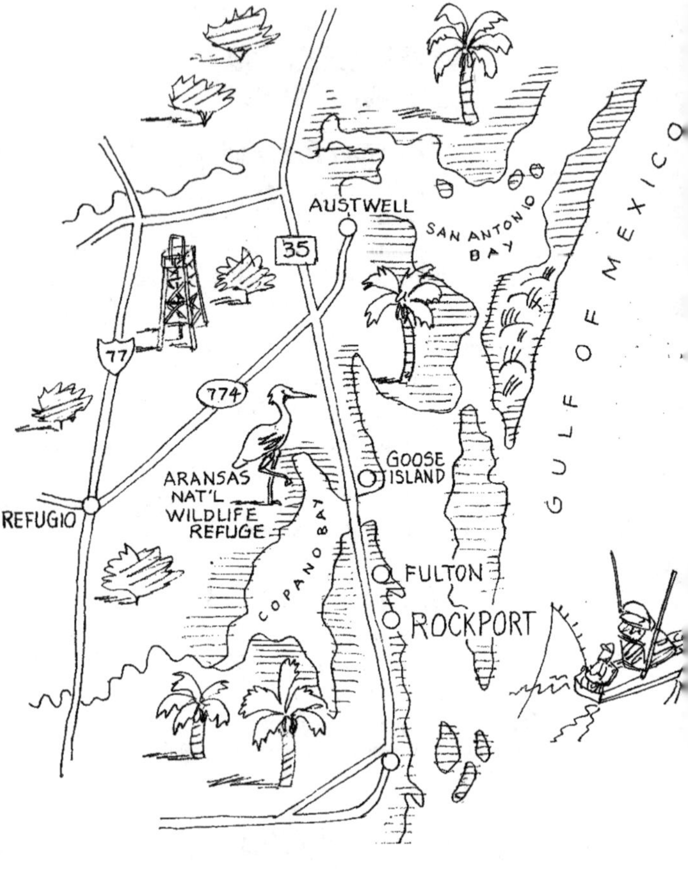

How many miles from Rockport to
- Austin 160
- Brownsville 195
- Corpus Christi 35
- Dallas 370
- Houston 180
- San Antonio 150

Chapter 4
WHAT'S FUN ABOUT ROCKPORT?

About Rockport	106
Aransas National Wildlife Refuge	107
Bird Watching Sites	108
Connie Hagar Cottage Sanctuary	110
Crabbing Sites	111
Demonstration Bird Gardens & Wetland Pond	112
Fulton Mansion State Historic Structure	113
Goose Island State Park	114
Golfing the Rockport Area	115
Lamar Cemetery and the Stella Maris Chapel	116
Rockport Beach Park	117
Rockport Center for the Arts	118
Sisters of Schoenstatt Shrine	119
Sport Fishing In Rockport	120
Texas Maritime Museum	123
"The Big Tree"	124
Whooping Crane Tours from Rockport	125
Touring Art Galleries	127
What's Kids' Stuff?	130
Watch for these Annual Events	131
Where to Eat?	133
Where to Stay?	135
Unique Places to Shop	140

What's Fun about  *Rockport?*

ROCKPORT

Rockport—a New England fishing village on the Texas coast, popular with folks wanting to leave cold climates for mild winters and reasonably priced accommodations.

This charming town has plenty to offer any family looking for a good time: quaint little shops, rows of fishing and sail boats, leaning windswept oak trees, fresh seafood, the famous "Big Tree," and the whooping cranes.

Rockport's main industries are tourism and commercial fishing, yet it also boasts having some of the best art galleries you'll find anywhere. If you love to fish, yet enjoy history, art, water sports, bird watching, and picnics, Rockport's the place for you.

The Rockport area includes the city of Fulton, home of the innovative cattle baron, George Fulton, whose mansion you'll want to tour. As the sign entering Fulton reads: "Welcome to Pirate Country—Home of the Oysterfest," this area once infested with pirates is now famous for its annual Oyster Festival.

See the rarest of birds, the whooping crane, now on the comeback after almost dying out as a species. Bay cruises to see these birds are available at Rockport Harbor from November through March.

Of course, no visit would be complete without seeing "The Big Tree." Some say it is over a thousand years old; others believe it to be twice that age.

I think you'll agree Rockport is exciting. Don't forget the camera!

What's Fun about Rockport?

ARANSAS NATIONAL WILDLIFE REFUGE

P. O. Box 100
Austwell, TX 77950-0100
512-286-3559

Famous for the Whooping Crane

Famous refuge on the Blackjack Peninsula—the winter home of the endangered whooping crane and one of the oldest refuges in our country. Visit their wildlife interpretive center museum and information center. Drive the 16-mile auto tour. Climb the observation tower or hike one of several trails.

You will find this experience very educational and come away with a better understanding of our migratory birds and sensitive ecosystems. These tidal marshes provide an abundant food supply for the survival of these birds.

Ask about the latest sighting of the whooping crane, which winters here from October through mid-April. Over 300 other species can be sighted at this refuge.

Plan to spend some time, wear comfortable shoes and clothes. Great photo opportunities.

Hours

Wildlife Interpretive Ctr . . . . 8:30am -4:30pm
Refuge . . . . Sunrise to sunset

Cost

Per car $2

Directions

Located 38 miles north of Rockport. Take Hwy 35 north to FM 774 and turn right. Follow the signs.

What's Fun about  Rockport?

BIRD WATCHING SITES

Rockport is a haven for birds

Rockport is a birding "hot-spot" with these birds of special interest: the least grebe, the white-tipped dove, the ferruginous pygmy-owl, the groove-billed ani, the buff-bellied hummingbird, the green kingfish, the pauraque, the couch's kingbird, the great kiskadee, the black-throated gray warbler, the tropical parula and the whooping crane.

The Rockport-Fulton Chamber of Commerce provides a "Birding Checklist and Guide" for $2. Stop and get a copy.

The Aransas National Wildlife Refuge, Demonstration Bird Gardens & Wetland Pond, Connie Hagar Cottage and Wildlife Sanctuaries, Goose Island State Park, and the Rockport Beach Park are excellent birding sites already mentioned in this chapter. Listed below are some other excellent places to go birding.

Copano Bay State Fishing Pier

The pier is on the Great Texas Coastal Birding Trail and is a well-known birding site for the American oystercatcher, hawks, raptors, loons, grebes, and ducks. Rare birds like the peregrine falcon, merlin, osprey, and swallowed-tailed kite have been seen flying around the pier.

What's Fun about  *Rockport?*

Fennessey Ranch Wildlife Tours
P.O. Box 99
Bayside, TX 78340
512-529-6600

Enjoy world-class birding and nature tours at this 4000-acre ranch that was once part of a 750,000 ranching empire dating back to a Spanish land grant in 1834. With over 1100 acres of wetlands and 9 miles of river frontage, it is a haven for numerous migratory birds, waterfowl and wildlife. The ranch offers country hayrides, wetland tours, hiking trails, scenic river trips, and more. Call for the schedule of activities. It is located 6 miles north of Refugio.

What's Fun about Rockport?

CONNIE HAGAR COTTAGE SANCTUARY

Friends of Connie Hagar
P. O. Box 586
Rockport, TX 78381-586

Visit a popular haven for birds

Land dedicated as a wildlife sanctuary in honor of Connie Hagar, who came here in 1934 to study the birds. Her husband Jack ran the Rockport cottages and their guests were some of the most well-known and respected ornithologists of their time, making Rockport an important place for birdwatching.

The cottages have long since vanished, but the land has been established as a bird sanctuary and historic site. The land consists of oak woodlands, native coastal grasses, and is a classic example of an oak motte habitat, all important to migratory birds.

Come walk the trails, observe the wildlife, and learn about this great legacy. Part of "The Great Texas Coastal Birding Trail."

Hours
Open any time

Cost
Free

Directions

On E. First and S. Church Streets, the entrance is on First Street. Take Loop 70 south through Rockport's business to S. Church St. Go left and continue to E. First and go right. Will be on the right.

What's Fun about  *Rockport?*

CRABBING SITES

It's the blue crab, callinectes sapidus, that's most edible along the Texas Coast. Identifying a blue crab is easy; it has a dark or brownish green abdomen, white lower legs, and bluish claws. You can tell a female crab by its red-tipped claws. The blue crab is a member of the "10-legged" decapod family: it has 2 claws, 6 walking legs, and 2 swimming legs in the rear. It thrives in a variety of environments—gulf waters, estuaries, salt flats, mouths of rivers, and brackish channels. It's a scavenger that lives on the muddy bottom, eating bits of vegetation and debris. The best time to go crabbing is April through October, until a cold snap sends them into deeper, warmer waters.

With a plentiful supply, crabbing is a popular sport in Rockport that requires very little equipment or skill. Try your luck at either Goose Island State Park or the Rockport Beach Park, two well-known places for catching crabs.

Crabs are fun to catch and easy to cook, but do require some effort to clean. Here is how to clean a crab. Twist off the claws and remove the "cone-shaped" apron on its underside by pulling it up and bending it back. Next, you remove the shell by inserting a thumb where you removed the apron and lifting it off. Now you wash out the gills, the organs and begin to remove the meat with a small knife—it will take some time. And of course, use a meat mallet or nutcracker to open the claws and leg.

What's Fun about Rockport?

DEMONSTRATION BIRD GARDENS & WETLAND POND

Native plants support wildlife

Experience a little heaven as you visit these unique and special gardens dedicated to the survival of hummingbirds, butterflies, and other beautiful birds.

These Demonstration Gardens show how we can cultivate beautiful native plants in our yards, around our businesses, and in our cities to support our ecosystem. Done effectively as it is here, it can be incorporated anywhere, not only along the Texas Coast. Come and borrow their ideas.

The effect this garden has on the way people garden is tremendous. Be sure to visit. Picnic area available.

Hours
Open any time

Cost
Free

Directions
On State Highway 35 North, before the WalMart Store, at the Texas Department of Transportation's rest area.

What's Fun about Rockport?

FULTON MANSION STATE HISTORICAL PARK

317 Fulton Beach Road
Fulton, TX
512-729-0386

Tour pioneering cattle baron's home

George Fulton built this beautiful home in 1874 with the same spirit of innovation that he used to run his cattle business.

Although George Fulton came to Texas too late to fight for Texas Independence from Mexico, he become a leader in the state's cattle industry. His home had the latest in technology and conveniences: modern indoor plumbing, central heating, and a gas lighting system.

Overlooking Aransas Bay, this fantastic three-story Victorian mansion must have seemed strange out on the Texas coast frontier but truly reflects the Fultons' progressive spirit and good taste.

Additional parking in the rear. Wheelchair accessible.

Hours

Wed. - Sun. .... 9am - 4pm

Cost

Adults $4
Children (over 6 & students) $2
Children (under 6) .... Free

Directions

On the corner of Henderson Street
and Fulton Beach Road.

What's Fun about Rockport?

GOOSE ISLAND STATE PARK

HC 04, Box 105
Rockport, TX 78382
512-729-2858 Reservations

Popular for camping and fishing

A fantastic 321-acre state park located in Aransas County, ten miles north of Rockport in conjunction with Copano, St. Charles, and Aransas Bay.

A great place to go camping. Facilities include RV and tent camping with electricity and water, a 160-foot fishing pier, a boat ramp, playgrounds, picnic areas, restrooms with showers, tables for cleaning fish, and a bait stand.

Activities available are fishing, boating, water-skiing, nature study, wildlife observation, photography, birdwatching, swimming, and a one-mile hiking trail through the woods. The famous whooping crane can often be seen from the fishing pier.

And best of all, this is the home of the "Big Tree." Whether you plan to stay here at Goose Island or not, it is well worth the visit to see this magnificent old tree.

Hours

Daily .... 8am - 5pm

Cost

Per Person $2
   (showers, tables for cleaning fish, & bait stand)

Directions

Ten miles northeast of Rockport on State Highway 35. Take State Highway 35 north of Rockport to Park Road 13. Go two miles east to the Park entrance.

What's Fun about  *Rockport?*

GOLFING THE ROCKPORT AREA

Three area golf courses

Rockport's mild winter climate makes golf a year-round sport.

ROCKPORT COUNTRY CLUB

101 Champions Drive • 512-729-4182

Open Tuesday through Sunday, this is a private 18-hole, full country club facility for USGA affiliated members only.

Greens fee (including cart)
Weekdays	$40
Weekends	$50

Winter Texan Special (one-month minimum)
Per person	$330
Per couple	$550

LIVE OAK COUNTRY CLUB

318 Country Club Road • 512-729-8551

Private course. Open Tuesday through Sunday, this 9-hole course features a clubhouse, driving range, swimming pool, and grill. Winter Texan specials.

Greens Fee .... Call for information

BUCCANEER BAY RESORTS

1024 8th Street • Lamar, TX 78382
512-790-8274

A new 9-hole public course near Goose Island State Park with country club facilities requiring membership. From Rockport, take Hwy. 35 South to Park Road 13 and go east.

Greens Fee $9

What's Fun about Rockport?

LAMAR CEMETERY AND THE STELLA MARIS CHAPEL

Chapel 512-729-2820 • 512-729-3387

Burial ground serving pioneers

Forgotten—this grand old cemetery was overgrown with weeds and bush until after World War II, when the Kroeger family needed to bury a family member and questioned its whereabouts. Even members of the community weren't sure of its location.

A cemetery association was organized, funds raised, and restoration began.

Here is the resting-place for many a pioneer and Confederate soldier. This one-acre cemetery dates back to 1838. You will find the grave of James W. Byrne, who purchased the land and laid out the townsite and cemetery. A historical marker was dedicated to the site on February 14, 1982.

The oldest structure and first church built in Aransas County, the *Stella Maris*—Star of the Sea—was built in 1858 from shell crete. It used to overlook Aransas Bay but was moved across from the cemetery in 1986. For more information about the cemetery and chapel visit the Aransas County Library.

Hours

Cemetery .... daylight
Chapel .... 1st & 3rd Sun. - 1 to 3pm

Cost Free

Directions

10 miles north of Rockport near
Goose Island State Park. Watch for signs.

What's Fun about Rockport?

ROCKPORT BEACH PARK

Sea Breeze Drive
Rockport, TX 78382
512-729-9392

City beach with fun activities

Popular with families because of all the fun activities it has to offer, one of the park's most attractive features is its mile-long sandy beach and saltwater pool. The kids will enjoy the playground. There are also picnic pavilions, volleyball courts, sailboat launching, exercise trails, a boat ramp, and paddleboats. During the summer, Jet Skis, beach umbrellas, and floats can be rented.

Rockport Beach is also a bird sanctuary. You can see numerous species of birds at any given time of the year. Observe them from the elevated observation platform.

Rockport is also a great place for fishing; there is a 360-foot shoreline pier, as well as an 800-foot fishing pier.

Hours

Daily .... 5am - 11pm

Cost

Per Person $3
3-day pass $5

Directions

Located in Rockport. Watch for signs along Business 35.

What's Fun about Rockport?

ROCKPORT CENTER FOR THE ARTS

902 Navigation Circle
Rockport, TX 78382
512-729-5519

Rockport's into art

The Rockport Art Association offers new exhibits monthly, displaying the talents of local artists in this beautiful old Victorian house, built in 1890 by Brian O'Connor.

Donated to the center in 1982, the house has been redesigned with studios, art galleries, a gift shop, and reception center.

Rockport has over 150 artists living in the area and 600 members in this association that was formed to promote art education and South Texas art, and to display quality work.

Hours

Tuesday – Saturday .... 10am – 5pm
Sunday .... 2pm – 5pm

Cost

Free; donations appreciated

Directions

In the blue Victorian house
next to Rockport Harbor.

What's Fun about Rockport?

SISTERS OF SCHOENSTATT CONVENT AND SHRINE

136 Front Street
Lamar, TX
512-729-1868

Active nunnery with authentic shrine

Seeking out a desirable location for their religious retreat, the Sisters moved to Lamar on Goose Island from Corpus Christi and created a haven for spiritual renewal and formation. Their main task is to further the Schoenstatt movement that began in Schoenstatt, Germany.

These sisters serve mankind as teachers, family counselors, social workers, and health-care workers.

Visit the authentic shrine, an exact replica of the one found in Schoenstatt, Germany, and one of many such shrines throughout the world.

Directions

Located on your way to Goose Island State Park.
Watch for signs.

What's Fun about Rockport?

SPORT FISHING IN ROCKPORT

Here are some good fishing guides and charters that I recommend for the Rockport area. As you can see, there are quite a few. Many provide everything you'll need except your food, drinks, and license. Call for further information.

Aransas Area Bay Fishing
512-729-1142

Bahia Rica Adventures
512-790-8833

Barry Badders Guide Service
512-727-0075 • 800-805-9997

Bay & Flats Fishing & Hunting Guides
512-729-9330

Gary Clouse Fishing & Hunting
512-729-1520 • 512-729-1550

Green Hornet Fishing Guide Service
512-790-9742 • 888-446-7638

Laguna Salada Safaris
512-729-9320 • 512-729-2010

Lone Angler Guide Service
512-729-2592

What's Fun about  *Rockport?*

Mark Williams Guide Service
512-729-7680

Nesloney Fishing & Hunting
512-729-7982

Norman Spears Guide Service
512-790-7342

Mike Sydows Fishing & Hunting
512-729-7212

Tecolote Charter Service
512-729-1529

Third Coast Adventures Guide Service
512-790-8341

Tightline Fishing Charters
512-729-6079

What's Fun about  *Rockport?*

FISHING PIERS

These are three very nice lighted fishing piers.
Another great way to fish!

Copano Bay State Fishing Pier

Five miles north of Rockport, along the Copano Causeway. Claims to be the longest fishing pier in the world. Once the original causeway across Copano Bay.
$1.75 for any fishing device.
Open 24 hours a day, weather permitting.
Bait, snacks, and drinks.

Fulton Fishing Pier

Along Fulton Beach at 350 Navigation Park
$1.50 per pole.
Snack bar, bait stand, gift shop.

Goose Island State Park Fishing Pier

In Goose Island State Park.
No charge for using the pier; however, there is a $2.00/person admission charge to enter the State Park.

What's Fun about Rockport?

TEXAS MARITIME MUSEUM

1202 Navigation Circle
Rockport, TX 78382
512-729-1271
512-729-6644

History of the Texas Gulf Coast

At this museum, you will learn the history of the Texas coast, from the Spanish and French explorers to our present-day oil and gas exploration.

See a permanent exhibit on Texas coast lighthouses, most of them built before the Civil War. At one time, there were 15, but only seven still stand today.

The museum also has a library for researching the Texas coast history.

Children will enjoy climbing aboard and exploring the ship's bridge. Visit the museum store for all kinds of nautical items and books.

Hours

Closed Monday

Tues. – Sat.	10am - 4pm
Sunday	1pm - 4pm

Cost

Adult	$4
Children (ages 12-4)	$2
Children (under 4)	Free

Directions

Across from the Rockport Harbor
on Business 35.

What's Fun about Rockport?

"THE BIG TREE"
Goose Island State Park

See this unique grand old tree

Your visit to Rockport must include this world-famous old live oak tree, estimated to be over a thousand years old. It is more than 35 feet in diameter, 44 feet in height, with a crown of 89 feet. Considered the largest tree in Texas.

Known by many different names, such as the "Lamar Oak," after the town of Lamar; the "Bishop's Tree;" from when a bishop lived nearby; and the "Goose Island Oak." It is simply referred to these days as "The Big Tree." Don't miss it!

Hours
Open during daylight hours

Cost
Free

Directions
In Goose Island State Park, 10 miles northeast of Rockport. Take State Highway 35 north of Rockport to Park Road 13. Go two miles east to the Park entrance. Watch for signs for the tree.

What's Fun about Rockport?

WHOOPING CRANE TOURS FROM ROCKPORT

Three excursion boats with great tours.

One of the most popular activities on the coast is to roam the bays in search of the famous endangered whooping cranes as they winter along the Texas coast. Aransas National Wildlife Refuge is home to magnificent creatures and touring by boat can be the best way to see them.

October through mid-April, sightseeing boats leave from Rockport Harbor, touring not only for the cranes, but also for dolphins and other species of birds. This is a great family activity.

The whooping crane, the rarest of birds, is making a comeback due to preservation efforts. In 1941, only 15 whooping cranes existed; today, there are over 150. Considered the tallest birds in North America, they are five feet high, with white bodies and jet-black wing tips. These birds love to feed on crabs, frogs, large insects, and crayfish. But they seldom eat fish, which is the reason they love the tidal marches of the refuge.

Capt. Ted's
Sandollar Pavilion, Fulton, Texas
512-729-9589
800-338-4551

Reservations a must. Narrated tours with enclosed heated air-conditioned cabins. Complimentary continental breakfast, am & pm tours, Nov. 1 - March 31. $33.00 per person. Closed Tuesday.

What's Fun about  *Rockport?*

Capt. John Howell
Rockport Harbor
512-729-7525
800-245-9324

Narrated tours aboard the **Pisces** inside a heated/air-conditioned cabin. Beverages & snacks available. Adults, $25; Children under 12, $17. Senior and group discounts available. Daily tours.

MV Wharf Cat
Rockport Harbor
512-729-4855
800-782-BIRD

Narrated tours with enclosed heated, air-conditioned cabin and an upper deck and scopes. Binoculars for rent. Closed Monday and Tuesday. $25 for adults and $17 for children 12 years and younger.

What's Fun about Rockport?

TOURING ART GALLERIES

Rockport has been known as an art community for a long, long time. Listed here are many of the art galleries you will find, most within a short walking distance of each other, concentrated on Austin Street.

Copano Designs
Steve Russell Gallery
Highway 35 N. near airport • 512-790-9700
Features original prints of local artist.

Estelle Stair Gallery & Studio
406 S. Austin Street • 512-729-2478
Housed in oldest building in town.
Oils, watercolors, sculptures.

Frame of Mine Gallery & Frame
1010 Wharf Street • 512-729-0967
Features original artwork & prints, glass,
watercolors, and more.

Frames & Thangs
404 S. Austin Street • 512-729-7273
Exhibits new and known talent.

Hummingbird Studio
1210 Highway 35 S. • 512-790-9700
Beautiful stained glass and custom work.

Little Gallery
Cactus and 4th Street • 512-729-0246
Displays works of local artists,
paintings of local scenes.

What's Fun about  *Rockport?*

J. Verschoyle Working Studio
15 Front Street, Lamar • 512-729-7826
Features works of this award-winning artist.

Jesus Bautista Moroles Granite Studio
408 W. Sixth Street • 512-729-6747
Work of award-winning granite sculptor.
By appointment only.

Niche Gallery
415 S. Austin Street • 512-729-5196
Features stained glass, glass art.

Peregrine Gallery
404 S. Austin Street • 512-729-0844
A full-service gallery for any art lover.

Rockport Artists' Gallery
414 S. Austin Street • 512-729-0600
Features original artwork, jewelry, pottery,
and wood carvings.

Rockport Center for the Arts
902 Navigation Circle • 512-729-5519
Members' gallery. Workshops and classes offered year-round for adults and children.

What's Fun about  *Rockport?*

Simon Michael School and Gallery of Fine Art
510 E. King Street • 512-729-6233
Works of internationally known
and award-winning artist.

Tejas Gallery and Gifts
415 S. Austin Street • 512-729-4488
Works with Texas flair by 25 local artists.

Windway Studio-Gallery
404 S. Austin Street • 512-729-9366
Aqua-media paintings by prominent artist and
works by other artists of South Texas.

What's Fun about Rockport?

WHAT'S KIDS' STUFF?
Take the kids to these places

Aransas Wildlife Refuge

Two simple games offered at the interpretive center will entertain children while they learn about the refuge's wildlife.

Game #1: Count the stuffed birds in the exhibits. Tell one of the staff members behind the counter how many you find. The number of birds on display makes it challenging; you may need to try again. Now take the auto tour; count how many birds you can see on the refuge.

Game #2: In the children's section, there is a hands-on display that allows them to touch animal related objects, like a turtle shell, and guess what animal it belongs to.

Goose Island State Park

Hike through the trees; play at the playground. Offers camping, fishing, picnicking, and crabbing.

Rockport Beach Park

The kids will love to go here for the beach, the slides, and the swings. Go birding, crabbing, fishing, or rent Jet Skis.

Rockport Center for the Arts

Offers art class such as watercolor, oil, drawing, stained glass, and more for children.

Texas Maritime Museum

The museum has a children's section with a full-size ship's bridge to explore.

What's Fun about Rockport?

WATCH FOR THESE ANNUAL EVENTS

Great events—you'll want to be there! Family oriented and eductional, too. Rockport offers many other events, but these are particularly wonderful to attend.

Fiesta in La Playa
P.O. Box 2334
Rockport, TX 78381
512-729-2063

Eight thousand people attend this event held in September, which features Tejano concerts, a mariachi band, arts & crafts, and good food.

Fulton Oysterfest
P.O. Box 393
Fulton, TX 78358
512-729-2388

A celebration of the oyster industry held in March at Navigation Park. Plenty of good food, entertainment, arts, crafts, and an oyster-eating contest. Approximately 30,000 attend this event.

Hummer/Bird Celebration
404 Broadway
Rockport, TX 78382
512-729-6445

The original migrating bird celebration sponsored every September by the Chamber of Commerce. Sets the standard for all other birding festivals in the state. Informative, educational programs.

What's Fun about  Rockport?

Rockport Art Festival
P.O. Box 987
Rockport, TX 78381
512-729-5519

Held in July, around the 4th. A weekend of beautiful works of art: watercolor, wood carvings, pottery, and more. Great to attend.

Rockport Seafair
P.O. Box 2256
Rockport, TX 78381
512-729-1522

Held in October. Experience the freshest in seafood, live entertainment, arts and crafts. Don't miss the crab races.

What's Fun about  *Rockport?*

WHERE TO EAT?
The Best Places to Eat in Rockport

I have listed for you the seven best places to eat out in Rockport. Each one serves good food, has a good family atmosphere, and is unique to the area. Price wasn't necessarily a consideration.

Back 40 Restaurant
Highway 35 N.
512-729-3478
Serves breakfast, lunch, and dinner.
Salad bar, steaks and seafood.
Open 7 am - 9 pm; Fri. & Sat. til 9:30 pm.

Chandler House Tea Room
801 Church St. (Loop 70)
512-729-2285
Ladies' favorite for lunch. Good breads, soups, salads, sandwiches. Gourmet coffee & tea.
Open Tues. - Sat. 11:30 am - 2:30 pm.

Crab-N Restaurant
Highway 35 S.
City By The Sea
512-758-2371
Freshest seafood around. Overlooks the   canal. Steaks, seafood, and more.

What's Fun about  *Rockport?*

Sandollar Pavilion Restaurant
Fulton Beach Road
512-729-8909

Considered the best place to eat in the Rockport area. Good seafood, steaks, salad bar, burgers, and more. Great atmosphere, back opens onto the water with huge windows and a patio. Open for breakfast, lunch, and dinner.

The Big Fisherman
Highway 188
512-729-1997

Favorite with Winter Texans, offering $1.99 chicken fried steak every Tuesday. Seafood, steak, salad bar, chicken, and more. Open Sun-Thur. 11 am-9:30pm, Fri. & Sat. 'til 10:30pm.

The Boiling Pot
Fulton Beach Road
512-729-6972

Casual dress, eat off paper-covered tables with no plates. Seafood dump. Good food. Patio. Across the street from Fulton Beach.

Open Mon.-Thur. 4pm - 10pm, Fri. & Sun. noon - 11pm, and Sat. 11am - 11pm.

Valenari's Restaurant
105 N. Austin Street
512-727-0717

Gourmet Italian food and a casual atmosphere. Open Wed. & Sat. 4pm - 'til crowd goes, Thurs. - Sun. 4pm - 10pm.

What's Fun about Rockport?

WHERE TO STAY?

The Best Places to Stay in Rockport

Here are what I consider to be the best motels, hotels, condos, bed & breakfasts, RV parks, and campgrounds. They all cater to families.

HOTELS, MOTELS, CONDOS

AAA Village Inn
503 N. Austin Street, Rockport, TX 78382
512-729-6370 • 800-338-7539

Bayfront Cottages
3095 Fulton Beach Road, Fulton, TX 78382
512-729-6693

Best Western Inn By The Bay
3902 Highway 35 N., Fulton, TX 78358
512-729-8351 • 800-235-6076

Days Inn Rockport
1212 E. Laurel, Rockport, TX 78382
512-729-6379 • 800-Days-Inn

Holiday Inn Express
901 Highway 35 N., Rockport, TX 78382
512-727-0283 • 888-727-2566

Hunt's Castle
725 S. Water Street, Rockport, TX 78382
512-729-2273

Kontiki Beach Resort Motel
2292 N. Fulton Beach Road, Fulton, TX 78382
512-729-4975 • 800-242-3407

What's Fun about  *Rockport?*

Laguna Reef Hotel/Suites
1021 Water Street, Rockport, TX 78382
512-729-1742 • 800-248-1057

BED & BREAKFASTS

The Rockport area has eight bed & breakfasts and they're all great. Some specialize in nature tours, others in history.

Anthony's by the Sea
732 S. Pearl Street, Rockport, TX 78382
800-460-2557 • 512-729-6100

Blue Heron Inn
801 Patton Street, Rockport, TX 78382
512-729-7526

Cayman House (Nature)
5030 Highway 35 N., Rockport, TX 78382
P.O. Box 160, Fulton, TX 78358
512-790-8884

Chandler House (History)
801 S. Church St., Rockport, TX 78382
512-729-2285 • 800-843-1808

Cygnet (Nature)
1450 Weeping Willow, Rockport, TX 78382
512-729-7009

What's Fun about  *Rockport?*

Hoopes' House (History)
417 N. Broadway, Rockport, TX 78382
800-924-1008 • 512-729-8424

Hummingbird Lodge
And Education Center (Nature)
5652 FM 1781, Fulton, TX 78382
888-827-7555 • 512-729-7555

The Habitat (Nature)
164 4th Street, Lamar, TX 78382
512-729-2362

RV PARKS AND CAMPING

All allow pets, many have swimming pools, tent camping, fishing piers, recreational activity rooms, and are handicap-accessible. Goose Island State Park is my favorite.

Bahia Vista R.V. Park
5801 FM 1781, Fulton, TX 78382
512-729-1226

Beacon R.V. Park
301 S. Fulton Beach Road, Fulton, TX 78382
512-729-3906

Circle W. R.V. Park
1401 Smokehouse Road, Rockport, TX 78382
512-729-1542

What's Fun about Rockport?

Goose Island State Park
Park Road 13, Lamar, TX 78382
512-389-8900 • 512-729-2858

Lagoons R.V. Park
600 Enterprise, Rockport, TX 78382
512-729-7834

Ocean Hideaway R.V. Park
3725 FM 1781, Rockport, TX 78382
512-729-1994

Shady Oaks R.V. Park
1301 Smokehouse Road, Rockport, TX 78382
512-729-6511

Sleepy Hollow R.V. Park
1701 16th St., Rockport, TX 78382
512-729-7390

Trailer Inn By The Bay
1371 Fulton Beach Road, Fulton, TX 78382
512-729-5608

Wateredge R.V. Park
717 N. Fulton Beach Road, Fulton, TX 78382
512-729-1100

What's Fun about  Rockport?

CAMPING

Here are some nice places to camp: they all include water, electricity, and huge oak trees. Once again, Goose Island State Park is the best.

Ancient Oaks Campground
1222 Highway 35 S., Rockport, TX 78382
800-962-6134 • 512-729-5051

Big Tree Trailer Inn & Cottage
130 Lamar Beach Road, Lamar, TX 78382
512-729-1541

Goose Island State Park
Park Road 13, Lamar, TX 78382
512-389-8900 • 512-729-2858

Woody Acres Trailer Park
1202 Mesquite, Fulton, TX 78382
512-729-5636

What's Fun about  Rockport?

UNIQUE PLACES TO SHOP

Austin Street's quaint little shops are a must when visiting Rockport. Below are others you may find interesting and unusual.

Enterprise Boutique

400 C. Enterprise Blvd.
512-729-2531

This shop is located at Enterprise and FM 2165, near the post office. Everything is handmade: linens, wearable art, glass hummingbirds, quilts, and more.

Rockport Center for the Arts Gift Shop

902 Navigation Circle
512-729-5519

This small gift shop has unique items: glassware, gifts items, cookbooks, regional books, and more. Admission to the center is free.

The Maritime Museum Shop

1202 Navigation Circle
512-729-6644

Inside the Texas Maritime Museum, the admission to the shop is free. The shop carries many maritime items, gifts and T-shirts.

PORT ARANSAS AREA

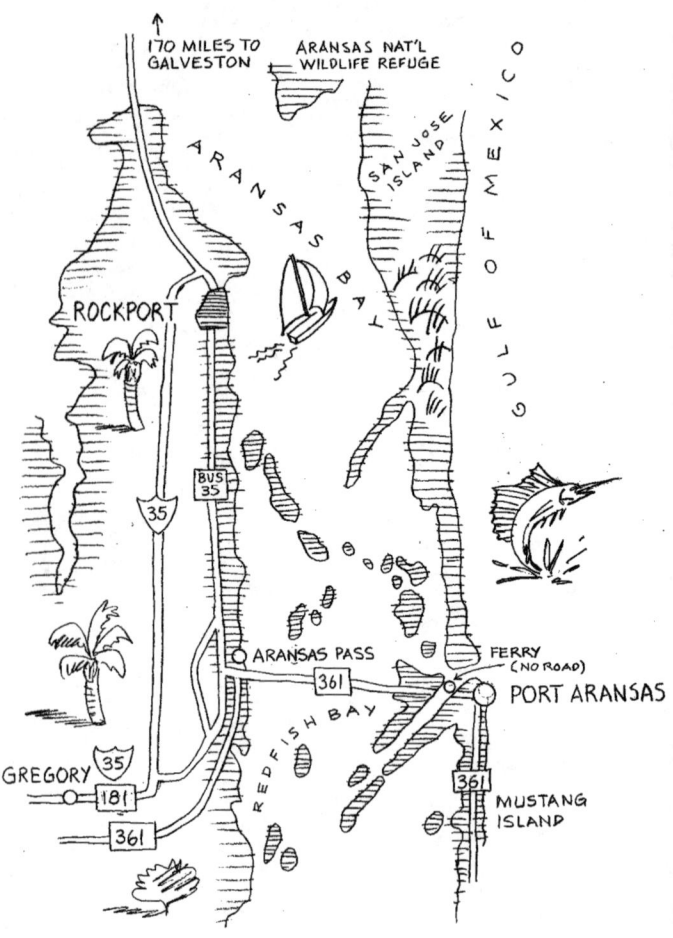

Chapter 5
WHAT'S FUN ABOUT PORT ARANSAS?

About Port Aransas	144
Aransas Lighthouse	146
Art Galleries	147
Bird Watching Sites	148
Fishing Docks and Marinas in Port Aransas	150
Fishing Piers and Jetties	151
Mustang Island State Park	152
Mustang Island Stables	153
Port Aransas Has Talent	154
Riding the Ferry to Port Aransas	155
San Jose Island Jetty Boat	156
Sea Shelling in Port Aransas	157
Sport Fishing in Port Aransas	158
University of Texas Marine Science Institute	161
Whooping Crane Tours	162
Watch for these Annual Events	163
Where to Eat?	165
Where to Stay?	166
Unique Places to Shop	169

What's Fun about Port Aransas?

PORT ARANSAS

Port Aranas—our own "Treasure Island." The pirate Jean Lafitte inhabited these islands in the 1820's and left behind tales of buried treasures. What we find is an island of many treasures. Port Aransas' year-round warm climate and excellent fishing make it a popular tourist destination. Its wonderful seafood restaurants and cozy accommodations add to the list of treasures people come for. Enjoy horseback riding on the beach, jet skiing, beach volleyball, beach combing, kite flying, wind surfing, bird watching, crabbing, camping, and relaxing. Folks in "Port A" enjoy life at a nice pace.

This onetime remote fishing village is located on the northern tip of Mustang Island, a barrier island 18 miles long and named after the wild horses left by the early Spanish explorers. It was called Port Aransas around 1910. Before that, it was known as Roperville in the 1890's and Tarpon in 1899. A hurricane completely destroyed the town in 1919.

Fishing is spoken in Port Aransas. Whether you like your "catch of the day" on your hook or on your plate, Port Aransas is where to do it. It is known as the "Fishing Capital of Texas." Deep-sea fishing is popular.

Not only is Port Aransas an excellent place to go fishing, this area is one of the National Audubon Society's top three picks for bird watching for the Texas Coast. Be sure to visit the Birding Center, home to hundreds of native and migratory species. This is a great family activity.

Port Aransas has two distinct landmarks, the Port Aransas Lighthouse and the Tarpon Inn. The lighthouse was built in 1854 and still functions. The Tarpon Inn was built in 1886, but it was rebuilt twice after a fire and a

 *What's Fun about Port Aransas?*

hurricane destroyed it. This famous inn once housed Franklin D. Roosevelt while he was fishing in Port Aransas. Look for his tarpon scale tacked to the inn's wall. Visitors are welcome.

You'll find a lot to enjoy about Port Aransas. Hope you catch a big one.

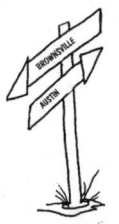

How many miles from Port Aransas to
- Austin 222
- Brownsville 189
- Corpus Christi 30
- Dallas 407
- Houston 237
- San Antonio 173

What's Fun about  *Port Aransas?*

ARANSAS LIGHTHOUSE

Imagine owning your own lighthouse

Built in 1854, the Aransas Lighthouse is the only lighthouse on the Texas Coast that's still operating, helping incoming ships find the ship channel's entrance. Now privately owned, this well-known landmark can best be seen by boat. Rich in history, the lighthouse's tower was severely damaged during the Civil War when Confederate Soldiers attempted to blow it up with dynamite. The lenses were buried to keep them from Union forces. After the war (in 1867) the tower was rebuilt and restored. The original light, a kerosene lamp, is now replaced with a 500-watt electric light. The lighthouse has a four-foot thick brick base and 69 wedge-shaped steps that spiral up to the light. Not open to the public.

What's Fun about  *Port Aransas?*

ART GALLERIES

You'll find artwork depicting the Texas Coast and the South, as well as works of nationally known artists. Port Aransas' art galleries are few, yet worth a visit.

Art Center for the Islands

309 N. Alister
Port Aransas, TX 78373
512-749-7334

An art center displaying members' artwork, such as stained glass, photography, sculpture, watercolors, oil paintings, and more. Offers art classes to the public.

Open Daily . . . . 11am - 5pm
Directions . . Next to Pelican's Landing Restaurant

Gary Osborne Fine Art

345 N. Alister
Port Aransas, TX 78373
512-749-6982
800-867-2248

Beautiful original artwork of museum quality by internationally well-known artists. Oil paintings, watercolors, bronzes, metal sculptures, handcrafted furniture, unique crafts and more. Be sure to see paintings by Kent Ullberg and Dalhart Windberg, two favorite artists.

Open Daily . . . . 11am - 5pm
Directions. . Next to Pelican's Landing Restaurant

What's Fun about  *Port Aransas?*

BIRD WATCHING SITES

You'll enjoy birding in Port Aransas, one of our country's top bird watching areas and one of the National Audubon Society's top three picks for the Texas coast. Of the 800 bird species found in North American, over 400 reside in the Port Aransas area sometime during the year. Here are two popular birding sites also on the **Great Coast Birding Trail** with vegetation that attracts numerous hummingbirds in the spring and fall.

Port Aransas Birding Center
Ross Avenue (off Cut-Off Road)
512-749-5307

Home to hundreds of bird species, native and migratory. See such birds as the buff-bellied hummingbird, seaside sparrow, white-tailed hawk, least crebe, crested caracara, reddish egret, frigate birds, raptors, and numerous waterfowl. Also home to "Boots," the 6-foot alligator, turtles, nutria, and other wildlife.

Meet on Wednesdays at 9 am for a bird watching nature tour. Everyone's welcome, there's no charge, and it's lots of fun.

Hours
Open all the time

Cost
Free

Directions
At the Port Aransas Treatment Plant
on Ross Avenue

What's Fun about Port Aransas?

Port Aransas Wetlands Park
Port Aransas Parks and Recreations
512-749-4158
Observe wildlife from the boardwalk and gazebo.

Hours
Open any time

Cost
Free

Directions
On Highway 361
about ¼-mile south of Avenue G.

What's Fun about  *Port Aransas?*

FISHING DOCKS AND MARINAS IN PORT ARANSAS

Deep Sea Headquarters
416 W. Cotter • 512-749-5597
Party boats with concessions and private charters.

Dolphin Docks
300 W. Cotter
512-749-4188 • 800-393-3474
My favorite. Offers scuba diving charters, bay and gulf fishing.

Fisherman's Wharf
900 N. Tarpon
512-749-5448 • 800-605-5448

Offers the Scat Cat and Wharf Cat, two large air-conditioned, heated party boats with concessions, great for families. Scenic cruises on a catamaran, nature and whooping crane tours.

Sportsplex Marina
815 Trout Street
512-749-4088

Seafood market, bait, tackle, bay and gulf fishing for up to 6 people.

Woody's Sport Center
136 W. Cotter
512-749-5252

Neptune Charter—private charters for bay and gulf fishing. Aboard the Duke for dolphin and bird watching tours, boat rides. Board the Island Queen party boat for bay fishing.

What's Fun about  Port Aransas?

FISHING PIERS AND JETTIES

Station Street Pier
North end of Station Street
Fish in the Corpus Christi Ship Channel for redfish, trout, sheepshead, and mackerel. Restrooms. Free

Horace Caldwell Pier
At the end of Beach Street.
Concessions, bait, fee per person and rod.

Nueces County Pier
At the end of Port Street (unpaved)
at Charlie's pasture.
Fish the ship channel for flounder, trout, drum, red fish, or crab with nets. No facilities. Free.

South Jetty
At Roberts Point Park.
Some of the best fishing is along the jetties.

San Jose Island and North Jetty
(See page on San Jose Island Jetty Boats).
North Jetty can be excellent fishing.

What's Fun about Port Aransas?

MUSTANG ISLAND STATE PARK

Highway 361
Mustang Island, TX 78373
512-749-5246
512-389-8900 Reservations

One of the best places in the area for camping.

Herds of wild mustangs, brought here by the Spaniards, once roamed the grassland comprising this 37,000 acre park at the southern end of Mustang Island. The park offers a small RV park, wading, mountain biking, sunbathing, birding, jetty fishing, shaded shelters, dressing rooms with showers, a mile-and-half of beach camping (300 sites), and 48 regular campsites with electricity and water. Reservations are required for the regular campsites, but not for beach camping. Beach camping depending on weather and tide conditions, so be sure to call ahead. Swimming is not recommended due to undercurrents.

Office Hours
Park closed at 10pm except for overnight guests.

Daily
8am - 5pm

Cost
Per person (12 yrs +) per day $3
Regular campsites $12
Beach camping $7

Directions
Located 14 miles southeast of Port Aransas.

What's Fun about Port Aransas?

MUSTANG ISLAND STABLES
Highway 361
Mustang Island, TX 78373
512-991-Ride
512-749-5055

Enjoy horseback riding along the beach

Enjoy taking the family horseback riding along the beach. Beginners are welcome. Open year-round. Early morning and evening rides are recommended during the hot months. Remember the bug repellent. Are there ten or more in your group? Make reservations for some additional beach activities, such as hayrides, weenie roasts, or a Texas barbecue. Fun!

Hours
Daily .... 9am - 5pm

Cost
(per hour horse riding)
Adults $20
Children 12 and under $15

Directions
One-and-a-half miles north of Mustang Island State Park or 7 miles north of Padre Island.

What's Fun about Port Aransas?

PORT ARANSAS HAS TALENT

Summertime fun in Port Aransas can include music and drama. Be sure find out what's happening when you're in town. Can be a great way to spend an evening in Port A.

Sunset Sounds
Port Aransas Parks and Recreation Programs
512-749-4111

Once a month, the amphitheater in Roberts Point Park features family musical entertainment. Bring a blanket or lawn chair to sit on.

Hours - First Thursday of each month
March - October 7pm
Cost .... Free
Directions .... Roberts Point Park

Port Aransas Community Theater
512-749-5340

Local performers stage summer productions at a local amphitheater on Cotter and White Streets (watch for sign). They like to perform a variety of shows, including children's plays and melodramas. Other times of the year, you will find them doing a dinner theater in various restaurants around town and plays at the Port Aransas Community Center. Call for show times and prices.

What's Fun about Port Aransas?

RIDING THE FERRY TO ARANSAS PASS
Ferry across the ship channel to Aransas Pass

Folks in the 20's wanted automobile access to Mustang Island from Aransas Pass. Today, over a million cars a year cross over the ship channel by ferry. The ferries (six in all), operate 24 hours, year-round, with peak season in June, July, and August when boarding may require a wait. Each ferry accommodates about 20 cars and can move approximately 100 cars an hour. Taking the ferry can be an enjoyable experience. You're likely to see dolphins, white and brown pelicans, and other wildlife, along with the usual flock of sea gulls. Watch for the Aransas Lighthouse on Harbor Island. Built in 1854, this famous landmark is still functioning. A one-way ferry ride across the channel takes approximately 5-10 minutes. Aransas Pass's Conn Brown Harbor is considered the "Shrimp Capital of Texas." It's home to the state's largest shrimping fleet. A great place to buy fresh seafood off the boats.

Hours
Operates 24 hours a day, year-round

Cost
Free

Directions
Pick up the ferry at the end of Cotter Street,
watch for signs.

What's Fun about  *Port Aransas?*

SAN JOSE ISLAND JETTY BOAT

P.O. Box 668
Port Aransas, TX 78373
512-749-5252

Take the jetty boat to an undeveloped island

Fishing can be excellent on "St. Joe's" and the North Jetty. San Jose Island is privately owned by a cattle rancher but open to the public for fishing, shelling, sunbathing, exploring, swimming, and surfing. There are no public facilities; bring your own food, water, tackle, and gear. San Jose Island is accessible only by boat. Passenger boats departing from Woody's Sport Center make ten trips daily to San Jose Island. Stay as long as you like, one-way boat trips take approximately 10 minutes.

Hours

10 trips daily................... 6:30am - 6pm

Cost

Adults $8.95
Children under 12 .... $4.95

Directions

San Jose is north of Mustang Island. The boat leaves from Woody's Sport Center, 136 W. Cotter Street.

What's Fun about  *Port Aransas?*

SEA SHELLING IN PORT ARANSAS

The undeveloped beaches on San Jose Island and Charlie's Pasture make shelling a popular pastime in Port Aransas. Once a month, the Port Aransas Parks and Recreations Department offers a beach walk with a local shell expert. This is a great family activity.

Beach Walk Adventures
512-749-4111

Join an expert for a guided walk on the beach. Offered on the 4th Friday, year round. Meet at Access Road 1 A. Free.

Charlie's Pasture

The locals recommend shelling Charlie's Pasture, an area running parallel to the Corpus Christi Ship Channel. This area is popular for finding large quantities of seashells.

San Jose Island

Pedestrian traffic is limited, making San Jose an idea place to go shelling. Take the jetty boat from Woody's Sport Center over to the island. Remember that there are no public facilities, so plan accordingly. (See the page on San Jose Jetty Boat.)

What's Fun about  *Port Aransas?*

SPORT FISHING IN PORT ARANSAS

Fishing in Port Aransas is excellent year-round. Fish the bays for speckled trout, redfish, flounder, and drum. Port Aransas's specialty is deep-sea fishing. Fish for kingfish, ling, small shark, dolphin fish, snapper, sailfish, shark, grouper, and blue marlin.

CHARTER FISHING GUIDES AND PRIVATE BOAT CHARTERS

Affordable Offshore Fishing
Bay and Offshore Fishing 512-790-5944

Ala Cat Fishing Charters Offshore Fishing
512-749-6393 • 800-264-3539

Beacon Charter Service
Bay Fishing 512-749-4273

Bill Busters Sportfishing
Bay and Offshore Fishing 512-749-5223

Charlie's Guide Service
Bay Fishing 512-749-3231

Copeland's DBA (Adventurer)
Offshore Fishing 512-749-7464

Crystal Blue Charters
Bay Fishing/Bird Watching Tours
512-749-5904 • 800-920-0931

What's Fun about Port Aransas?

Elliott Guide Service
Bay Fishing 512-643-7351

Fishin' Fever
Bay Fishing 512-749-6957

Freespool and Ladyfish Charters
Bay and Offshore Fishing 512-749-6278

G & S Marine, Inc.
Scuba Diving, Service Boat, and Fishing
512-270-7292

Happy Bottoms Charters
Offshore Fishing 512-758-5316

Hook Guide Service
Bay Fishing 512-749-4925

Ironhead Charter Service
Offshore Fishing 512 949 0910

Investigator Fishing Charters
Offshore Fishing 512-776-5223

Marshall's Guide Service
Bay Fishing 512-749-6633

Private Deep Sea Charters
Offshore Fishing 512-749-7311

What's Fun about  *Port Aransas?*

Queen's Line, Inc.
Fishing, Sightseeing, Boat Rides, Nature Tours
Groups Welcome
512-749-5252 • 512-749-6969

Sailsman Charter Boat Services
Bay and Offshore Fishing
817-737-0833

Shallow Water Charters
Bay Fishing, Fly Fishing, Duck Hunting,
Bird Watching
512-749-6525

South of Reason Charters
Bay and Offshore Fishing
512-749-7543

Waterworld Charters
Offshore Fishing
512-749-3556

What's Fun about Port Aransas?

UNIVERSITY OF TEXAS MARINE SCIENCE INSTITUTE

750 Channelview Dr.
Port Aransas, TX 78373
(Visitor Center is on Conner Street)
512-749-6729

A marine biology research and educational facility with visitor center

At this facility you'll find a visitor center for educating the public about our wonderful marine environment. The visitor center has several aquariums on display featuring sea life in the Gulf of Mexico and some impressive past and current research projects. Take a self-guided tour of the exhibits, then enjoy the educational videos about our marine life in the auditorium, shown Monday through Thursday, 11am - 3pm. Well worth the visit and a fun activity for the family.

Hours

Winter Hours
Weekdays .... 8am - 5pm
Summer Hours include weekends
Saturday .... 9am - 5pm
Sunday............................ Noon - 4pm

Cost
Free

Directions
On Conner Street before you get to the beach, on your way to the ferry.

What's Fun about  *Port Aransas?*

WHOOPING CRANE TOURS

Port Aransas offers tours to see whooping cranes

Enjoy taking a narrated nature boat tour in search of the beautiful, endangered whooping cranes, wintering in the Aransas National Wildlife Refuge from October through mid-April. The whooping crane and other wonderful wildlife can best be seen when exploring coastal waters. Make reservations in advance.

The Wharf Cat
Fisherman's Wharf
P.O. Box 387
Port Aransas, TX 78373
512-749-5760 • 800-605-5448

Narrated tours aboard the **Pisces**, inside a heated or air-conditioned cabin with an upper deck with scopes. Beverages and snacks are available.

Hours
Mon & Tues. . . . . 10:30am & 3:30pm

Cost
(Senior and group discounts available)
Adults $25
Children 12 and under $17

Directions
The whooping crane tours depart from Fisherman's Wharf, 900 N. Tarpon Street.

What's Fun about  Port Aransas?

WATCH FOR THESE ANNUAL EVENTS

Port Aransas has fishing tournaments galore, one practically every weekend. (This is the "Texas Fishing Capital.") Below are some of the major annual events in Port Aransas. Do call the phone numbers listed for actual dates and more information or call the Chamber of Commerce, 800-452-6278.

Port Aransas Wild Game and Seafood Dinner (February)
800-242-3084

Presented by the Lion's at the civic center, a very popular wild game and seafood feast served buffet style.

Celebration of Whooping Cranes (March)
512-749-5911

Celebrates the whooping crane and other migratory birds with boat trips, nature cruises, workshops, seminars, photography, trade shows, and birding tours.

GCCA Take-A-Kid Tournament (June)
512-749-3252

Annual event fishing tournament involving children's participation.

Annual Deep Sea Roundup (July)
512-749-6339

Put on by the Boatman's Associations. Started in 1931. This is one of the oldest, largest, and most popular fishing tournaments, establishing Port Aransas as a center for sport fishing.

Outboard Fishing Tournament (July)
512-749-4429

A three-day event, limited to fishermen with outboard motor-powered boats and includes a captain's meeting dinner and two buffets.

E.M.S. Chili Cook-Off (September)
412-749-3545

Well-attended annual event at Robert's Point Park with a chili cook-off and Texas barbecue.

Shallow Water Roundup and Seafood Bash (November)
800-452-6278

Famous for the seafood feast after the tournament.

What's Fun about  *Port Aransas?*

WHERE TO EAT?

Best Places to Eat in Port Aransas

Beulah's
200 E. Cotter • 512-749-4888

Well-known restaurant generally requiring reservations. Fine dining outdoors on the veranda, weather permitting. Daily specials, serving dinner Wednesday through Sunday, also a Sunday Brunch.

Crazy Cajun
303 Beach Street • 512-749-5069

Cajun-style seafood such as crawfish, shrimp, gumbo, dirty rice, rice and beans, baby back ribs, and more. What's unique is how they serve the food, on butcher paper, family style. Live entertainment on weekends. Dinner only Monday - Friday. Lunch and dinner Saturday and Sunday.

Dockside Restaurant and Patio
440 W. Cotter • 512-749-4322

Breakfast, lunch, and dinner with daily specials.

Pelican's Landing Restaurant
337 N. Alister • 512-749-6405

My favorite will be yours, too. One of the best restaurants on the Texas coast, serving fresh, locally caught seafood. Offers steaks and other specialties. Dine outdoors on the covered deck, weather permitting. Open daily.

Trout Street Bar and Grill
104 W. Cotter

Dine overlooking the harbor. Daily lunch and dinner specialties. Serving seafood and black Angus beef.

What's Fun about  *Port Aransas?*

WHERE TO STAY?

Best Places to Stay in Port Aransas

Aransas Princess Condominiums
230 S. Cut-Off Road
512-749-5118 • 800-531-9225

A 112-unit complex with furnished 2 and 3 bedroom condos on the beach, 2 pools (one heated), fish room, Jacuzzi, tennis courts, shuffle board.

Cline's Landing
1000 N. Station Street
512-749-5274
Near the beach, 108 units, condos,
penthouse suites, pool.

Coral Cay Condominiums
1419 S. 11th Street
512-749-5111 • 800-221-4981
On the beach with 1, 2, and 3 bedroom condos, 2 pools, new tennis courts,

Dunes Condominiums
1000 Lantana
512-749-5155 • 800-288-DUNE
Condos on the beach with view, pool, tennis courts and volleyball, Jacuzzi, and health club.

Mayan Princess Condominiums
901 9th Street
512-749-5183 • 800-662-8907
Sixty-unit complex with furnished condos on the beach, washer/dryer, tennis courts, and 3 pools.

What's Fun about  *Port Aransas?*

Port Royal Ocean Resort
6317 SH 361
512-749-5011 • 800-242-1034

Personally my favorite, a 210-unit complex with furnished 1, 2, and 3 bedroom condos, 4 heated hot tubs, huge swimming pool, room service, fishing, horse riding, and restaurant.

Sandcastle Condominiums
800 Sandcastle Dr.
512-749-6201 • 800-727-6201

A 180-unit complex with 1, 2, and 3 bedroom condos on the beach with boardwalk, pool, tennis and basketball courts.

Sea Sands Condominiums
1421 S. 11th Street
512-749-6246

Fourty-units with condos near the beach with pool.

Tarpon Inn
200 E. Cotter
512-749-5555 • 800-365-6784

A historic landmark with 24 units near the beach, fishing docks, shopping, porches with rocking chairs and a fine dining restaurant. No television or phones. Offers relaxation and sanity.

MOTELS

Alister Square Inn
122 S. Alister
512-749-3000 • 888-749-3003

Fifty units with refrigerators, microwaves, pool, TV, handicapped facilities, and a good location.

What's Fun about Port Aransas?

Best Western Ocean Villa
400 E. Ave. G.
512-749-3010
Three blocks from the beach, TV, kitchenettes.

RV PARKS AND CAMPING

Island RV Resort
700 6th Street
512-749-5600

Has 199 RV and tent camping, pool, hot tub, bath house, recreation room, 5 blocks from the beach and 2 blocks from the grocery store.

Mustang Island State Park
Highway 361, Mustang Island
512-749-5246
512-389-8900 Reservation

Located 15 miles south of Port Aransas with 48 RV spaces and camping sites with electricity and water. Also beach camping. Very nice.

Pioneer RV Park
120 Gulf Wind Dr. (Hwy 361)
512-749-6248

Largest and newest RV resort with 211 RV spaces, recreation and meeting room, pool, bath house, fish cleaning facilities, bird watching, general store, laundromat, cable and phone.

What's Fun about  *Port Aransas?*

UNIQUE PLACES TO SHOP

Absolutely Everything Under the Wave
314 E. Ave. G.
512-749-4738

Offers a wide variety of items from 18-hole miniature golf, gift shop, souvenirs, beach inflatable toys, to a food grill.

Fly it Port "A"
Avenue G and 10th Street
512-749-4190
Kite shop with windsocks and fun toys.
Open daily 10am - 6pm.

Port A, U.S.A. Shops
337 Alister
Art gallery, boutique gifts shops, and the art center for the Island.

Fish Tales (Port A, U.S.A.)
345 N. Alister
512-749-4733
Clothing, jewelry, and gift items.

Silver Fox Trading Company
221 Beach Street
512-749-4899
Unusual handcrafted gifts, jewelry, charms, Indian jewelry, and beads.

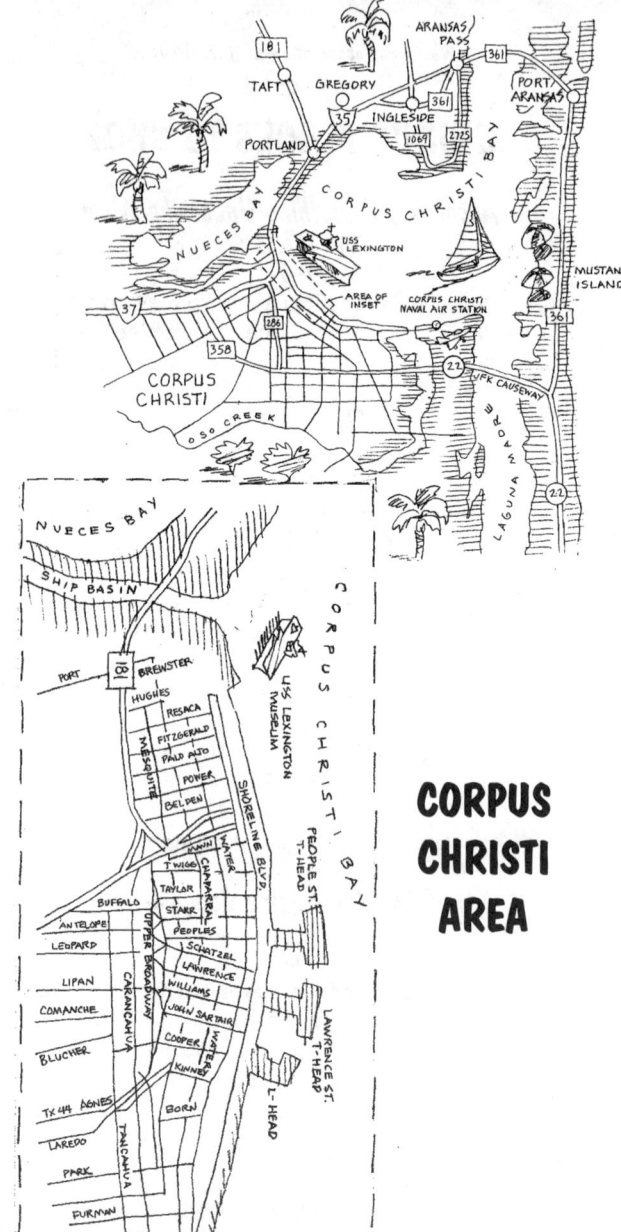

CORPUS CHRISTI AREA

Chapter 6
WHAT'S FUN ABOUT CORPUS CHRISTI?

About Corpus Christi	172
Art Center of Corpus Christ	174
Asian Cultures Museum & Education Center	175
Bird Watching	176
Botanical Gardens	179
Captain Clark's Narrative Cruises	180
Centennial House	181
Christmas House	182
Corpus Christi Greyhound Racing	183
Golfing in the Corpus Christi Area	184
Harbor Playhouse	186
Heritage Park	187
International Kite Museum	188
King Ranch	189
Naval Station Ingleside	192
Padre Island National Seashore	193
South Texas Institute for the Arts	194
Sport Fishing in the Coastal Bend Area	195
Texas State Aquarium	199
The World of Discovery	200
USS Lexington	201
Waterfront Art Market & Art Galleries	202
Watch for these Annual Events	203
What's Kids Stuff?	206
Where to Eat?	207
Where to Stay?	209
Unique Places to Shop	213

What's Fun about Corpus Christi?

CORPUS CHRISTI

Corpus Christi —Texas' Riviera. Discovered in 1519 by Spanish explorer Alanzo de Pineda, who named the bay "Corpus Christi" after the Feast of the Body of Christ. Fierce Indians chased the Spanish away.

The first permanent settlement started in 1839 when Henry L. Kinney reportedly left for the frontier to get over a failed love. He started Kinney's Trading Post, which became an important means of supply during the Civil War.

Early homes and buildings were made of shell crete, a mixture of burnt shells, sand, and quicklime. See evidence of this in the Centennial House, Corpus' oldest existing house, built in 1849.

The city's potential as a resort was first realized during the Civil War. Clean air, beaches, and water sparkling make Corpus paradise for any family on vacation.

Stroll the famous seawall designed by Gutzom Boregham, the same man who carved Mount Rushmore.

Notice the striking art museum designed by the award-winning architect Philip Johnson, who also created the famous for Pennzoil Place in Houston.

Park the car, then take the pedestrian walk across the Harbor Bridge, being careful of the traffic. The view of the bay, the Corpus Christi Port, and the city makes for a spectacular sunset. Bring binoculars; this is birders' country.

Enjoy another view of Harbor Bridge from the Watergarden in Bayfront Arts and Science Park, a lovely area with a huge circular fountain that brings relaxation and peace to any soul soaking up the fantastic view.

You must drive along Ocean Drive, lined with palms and stately homes. Continue your drive (it takes two

What's Fun about Corpus Christi?

hours) over the JFK Causeway to Padre Island, then go up Mustang Island to Port Aransas, across the channel (by way of the free, state-operated ferry) to the mainland again, then return via State Highways 35 and 181. Fun! Fun! Fun!

Corpus' beaches, climate, and hospitality, along with her three biggest attractions—the USS Lexington, the World of Discovery, and the Texas State Aquarium—are among the many reasons to come here.

Visit Selena's gravesite in a city where a tragedy like this seldom, if ever, occurs. See the monument erected to her memory on Shoreline Drive in front of the T-Head.

A must is the guided tour at the King Ranch. Very impressive, and one of the best tours I have ever been on. The King family gives us a real pioneer legacy and is famous worldwide.

Corpus Christi has it all: endless beaches, fresh seafood, birds, fish, heritage, and culture, and a peaceful serenity. On a recent visit, I ordered shrimp at the Water Street Seafood Company Restaurant and can't say enough about their food. Experience it for yourself.

Hope you look forward to going.

How many miles from Corpus to

Austin	218
Brownsville	159
Corpus Christi	230
Dallas	413
Galveston	230
Houston	215
San Antonio	144
Mexico (via Brownsville)	159
Mexico (via Larado)	141

ART CENTER OF CORPUS CHRISTI

100 Shoreline Blvd.
Corpus Christi, TX 78401
512-884-6406

A showcase for local and area artists

It is a "working" center with an informal atmosphere. In addition to the Main Gallery where exhibits are changed monthly, the 14,000 sq. ft. building houses artis-int-residence studios and classrooms where demonstrations and workshops are regularly scheduled.

Art Center Hours

Tues.-Sat. .... 10am - 4pm

Gift Shop and Restaurant hours:
Tues-Fri. .... 11am - 4pm
Saturday .... 11am - 2pm

Art Center Cost
Free

Directions
In the heart of the city, on the bayfront.

What's Fun about Corpus Christi?

ASIAN CULTURES MUSEUM & EDUCATIONAL CENTER

1809 N. Chaparral Street
Corpus Christi, TX 78401
512-882-2641

Experience Asian Culture

Established in 1974, this unique Asian Museum was the first of its kind in South Texas. The founder, Mrs. Billie Trimble Chandler, taught school in Okinawa, the Philippines, and Japan for 17 years and wanted to share her experiences with Americans.

The Center provides educational opportunities that bridge these diverse cultures.

It includes fascinating displays and exhibits such as dolls made from special clay found in Hakata, Japan, a Chinese cinnibar, and a Filipino Sunka Board. Popular with school groups and a great place to take the family, the Museum also sponsors Asian festivals throughout the year.

Hours

Tues.-Sat .... 10am -5pm

Cost

Adult	$4
Senior (60+) & Military	$3.50
Children (ages 6-12)	$2.50
Children (under 5)	Free

Directions

Near the Bayfront Arts and Science Park
(next to World of Discovery Museum).

What's Fun about Corpus Christi?

BIRD WATCHING SITES

Some of the best bird watching in the country

You don't have to leave Corpus Christi to find birds. At the **T-Heads and Cole Park,** on Shoreline and Ocean Drives, you can see pelicans, ducks, sandpipers, and cormorants. **Corpus Christi State University**, on the 6300 block of Ocean Drive, attracts curlews, sandpipers, and plovers. Blucher Park, next to the Central Library, is a great place to spot migrating hummingbirds and passerines. Every weekend in April (except Easter), guided tours begin at 7:30 am at the 100 block of Carrizo Street.

John F. Kennedy Causeway between Corpus Christi and North Padre Island also offers a great view of shoreline birds, herons, egrets, and rookery islands. Be aware of heavy traffic; park on sandy shoulder and be sure to bring your telescopes and binoculars.

Listed below are other sanctuaries, refuges, state parks, beaches, and "hot spots" for observing birds. As many as 500 species make this area their home some time during the year, but the best time for seeing most of them is in the winter months—mid-October through mid-April.

Hazel Bazemore County Park

Bluebirds in winter, owls, paurague, warblers, and other passerines, humingbirds, shore birds. Great viewing of spring and fall migration. Brushy wooded park on the Nueces River. Entrance from Hwy 624, 1/2 mile west of Hwy 77S.

Choke Canyon State Park

Open from 8am-5pm daily. See nesting swallows, turkey, caracaras, titmice, thrashers, wrens. Take Exit 69 from IH-37 north, turn left onto State Highway 72 and follow the signs.

Fred Jones Nature Sanctuary

A privately owned sanctuary. Take Moore Ave. (893) west of Portland about 6 miles and go left on County Rd 69 east, 1/2 mile on left, watch for sign.

Hans A. Suter Wildlife Area

One of the best birdwatching locations in Texas. Nature park with boardwalk on the western shore of Cayo del Oso. Open year-round and home to white pelicans, shorebirds, egrets, gulls, herons, and a number of other avian inhabitants favoring the coastal marshland climate. Enter from Ennis Joslin Road.

Hilltop Community Center

Native brush habitat with trails. Open during daylight hours. Located at 11426 Leopard St., across from the fire station and .3 miles west of Violet Rd.

Indian Point

Bayfront marshes and ponds. See migrants, skimmers, herons, egrets, rails, gulls, terns. Located at the north end of Nueces Bay Causeway, Hwy 181. Additional salt cedar and ponds on paved road to the north.

Lake Corpus Christi State Recreation Area & Wildlife Sanctuary

From IH-37, exit 34, take 359W for 5.5 miles. Turn right on Park Road 25 north. Sanctuary will be on the left. Park on road and stay on paths in isolated wooded, brushy area. Continue down road to park entrance. Swallows nest at dam. See cactus wrens, thrashers, verdins, hawks, owls.

Nueces River Park

Explore the wooded river, across river & adjacent to park. Daily 9am-5pm. Nueces River and Highway 77 at exit 16.

Packery Channel County Park

Oak mottes along the channel are popular with migratory birds. From JFK Causeway, take Park Road 22 one mile east.

Padre Island National Seashore and Bird Island Basin

Tourist fee; facilities. Shorelines of Gulf and Laguna Madre are good birding. Marshes along road are also good. Bird Island Basin is to the right of the main road. Watch for signs.

Rob and Bessie Welder Wildlife Refuge
512-364-2643

Located east off Hwy. 77 North on Ainron, 7.4 miles. Gate opens at 3 pm on Thursday for guided tours. Museum. Restrooms.

What's Fun about Corpus Christi?

BOTANICAL GARDENS

8545 S. Staples Street
Corpus Christi, TX 78413
512-852-2100

Displaying native plants, and wildlife

Within these 180 acres are nature trails, gardens, a bird observation tower, a visitor center, a gift shop, a picnic area, a children's garden, an art gallery, a playground, and much, much more.

Visit the Orchid House with over two thousand orchids along with plumeria, bromeliads, cycads, and fern.

The shady Bird and Butterfly Trail (markers identify plants along the way) leads to the observation tower for viewing egrets, white pelicans, ducks, and Roseate Spoonbills.

Coming soon are other attractions like a sensory garden that invites visitors to touch, smell, and feel particular plants.

Call in advance and make arrangements for a docent tour. Wear comfortable shoes and casual clothes. A jug of ice water is a good idea on a hot summer afternoon.

Hours
Closed Monday
Tues.-Sun. .... 9am - 5pm

Cost
Adults................................... $2
Children (ages 12-5) $1
Children (Under 5) .... Free

Directions
South of Oso Creek. Take Staples across creek as it turns into 2444.

CAPTAIN CLARK'S NARRATIVE CRUISES

Peoples Street T-Head, Slip #49
Corpus Christi, TX
512-884-8306

Scenic cruise of the bay and harbor

Take a one-hour narrated scenic cruise aboard the Flagship paddle wheeler of Corpus Christi Bay, the sixth-largest port in the United States. Enjoy the comfort of an air-conditioned viewing deck with plenty of concessions. The Flagship offers Saturday evening cruises complete with live music.

Scenic Cruise Hours

Winter
Daily (Closed Tuesdays).................... 3pm

Summer
Daily................. 11am, 1pm, 3pm, 7:30pm

Cost

Adults....................................... $7
Children (4 -11) $4
Children (3 & under) .... Free

Directions

Located at the Corpus Christi Marina on the Peoples Street T-head.

What's Fun about Corpus Christi?

CENTENNIAL HOUSE

411 North Broadway
Corpus Christi, TX
512-992-6003

House with a fascinating story

Built in 1849, this is the oldest existing house in Corpus Christi. It was used by the Confederate Army as a hospital during the Civil War and also served as a refuge from Indian raids, banditos, and treacherous storms. Come hear the stories.

Here is an excellent example of Classic Revival architecture. Anyone interested in history, architecture, or the Civil War will enjoy visiting this Classic Revival house, but don't stop here; there are nine other homes worth seeing in Heritage Park. Special tours for 10 people or more; call one week in advance.

Hours

Wednesday .... 2pm - 5pm

Cost

Adults	$2
Children (over 6)	$1
Children (under 6)	Free

Directions

On N. Broadway. Take Williams Street going east from Shoreline Drive (Williams turns into Lipan Street). On the corner of N. Broadway and Lipan.

What's Fun about Corpus Christi?

CHRISTMAS HOUSE
and Santa's Texas Workshop
Route 1 Box 82 A, Falfurrias, TX 78355-9604
512-325-2068 • 800-276-4339

Spirit of Christmas on a Texas ranch

You'll believe Santa moved to Texas when you visit Janie, Esther, and Dorothy Minten's Christmas House. These three sisters grew up with fond Christmas memories and love to decorate the family ranch house in splendid detail every year with a new theme.

A popular annual event for many tour groups, church groups, families, and Winter Texans. Open only for groups of 6 to 24 on weekdays and 6 to 36 on weekends with reservations from October through March. The tour takes 3 hours.

Visit Santa's Texas Workshop, with all kinds of Christmas items from simple ornaments to collectibles. The store is open year-round but doesn't keep regular hours. Call and let them know you are coming.

Hours

Mon. - Thurs.	9am and 1:30pm
Saturdays	9am, 2:30pm, 4pm
Sundays	1pm and 4pm

Cost

Adults & children (5 and older)	$7
Children (ages 2-4)	$5

Directions

Between Premont and Falfurrias. On Hwy 281 watch for a tall red and white tower with flashing lights on the east side. Go east 2 ½ miles on Jim Wells County Road 401.

What's Fun about Corpus Christi?

CORPUS CHRISTI GREYHOUND RACING

5302 Leopard Street
Corpus Christi, TX 78469
800-580-7223 • 512-289-9333

The sixth largest spectator sport in the U.S.

Watching dog races from this $21 million facility, a 60-acre park, can be a real treat. Considered one of the best in the U.S. Featuring a full-service food court with an excellent view of the track. Television sets at each table let you follow the action.

Hours

Open daily for matinee & evening races
(Call for current schedule)
Monday (Simulcast only)

Tues. - Sat.	11am
Wed., Sat. & Sun. Matinee	1:30

Cost

Clubhouse	$2
General	$1

Directions

Located on Leopard Street off of
IH-37 at Navigation.

What's Fun about Corpus Christi?

GOLFING IN THE CORPUS CHRISTI AREA

Municipal Golf Courses

If golf is your bag, swing by one of these eight courses and enjoy a great afternoon.

Alice Municipal Golf Course

North Texas Blvd. in Anderson Park • Alice
512-664-7033
Eighteen-holes, pro shop, driving range.
Green fees: $3.50 weekdays, $6.25 weekends.

Gabe Lozano Sr. Golf Course

4401 Old Brownsville Road • Corpus Christi
512-883-3696
Regular 18-holes and executive 9-holes. Greens fees vary with day. Open 7 days a week.

Kings Crossing Country Club

6201 Oso Parkway • Corpus Christi
512-994-1395
Winter Texas specials on 18-hole course. Green fees: $35 weekdays & $55 weekends.

L.E. Ramey Municipal Course

Hwy 77 South • Kingsville
512-592-1101
Eighteen-holes, pro shop, driving range, open daily.
Green fees: $3.50 weekdays, $6.75 weekends.

What's Fun about  *Corpus Christi?*

North Shore Country Club
801 E. Broadway (off Hwy 181) • Portland
512-643-2795

Eighteen-holes course, full country club facilities. Green fees: $45 Mon.-Thurs., $55 Fri. & Sat., includes golf cart.

Oso Beach Golf Course
5601 S. Alameda • Corpus Christi
512-991-5351

Eighteen-holes course, pro shop, snack bar. Green fees: $9 weekdays, $11 weekends.

Pharaoh Country Club
7111 Pharaoh • Corpus Christi
512-991-2477

Eighteen-hole course, full country club facilities, driving range, pro shop, restaurant. Green fees: $25 weekdays, $35 weekends & holidays.

Sinton Municipal Golf Course
Hwy 181 • Sinton
(Three miles north of Sinton)
512-364-9013

Eighteen-hole course, pro shop, driving range. Green fees: $7 weekdays, $8 weekends & holidays. Winter Texan specials. Open daily. (Closed 1st & 3rd Tuesday every month.)

What's Fun about Corpus Christi?

HARBOR PLAYHOUSE
1 Bayfront Park
Corpus Christi, TX 78401
512-888-7469
512-882-3356 tickets

Corpus Christi's community theater

This charming theater located by the sea seats 474 people and claims to be Texas' oldest continually performing community theater. Offers musicals, dramas, comedies, children's shows, and summer melodramas.

Hours
(Call for shows and times)
Box office hours
Mon. - Sat. .... Noon - 6pm

Cost
Tickets range from $10 - $12

Directions
At the Bayfront Arts and Science Park,
next to the World of Discovery Museum.

What's Fun about  *Corpus Christi?*

HERITAGE PARK

(Multicultural Center)
1600 Chapparal Street
512-883-0639

Nine beautiful turn-of-the-century homes.

Lichtenstein House (1905)
Sidbury House (1893)
Gugenheim House (1905)
Littles-Martin House (1900 - 10)
Galvan House (1908)
Grande-Grossman (1904)
Merriman Bobys House (1851)
Jalufka House (1901)
McCampbell House (1908)

Take a self-guided walking tour featuring these restored, turn-of-the-century homes situated on one square block in Corpus Christi. Maps and details about the homes are available at the Galvan House. There are also a tea room and gift shop on the grounds. Tours with guide can also be arranged at the Galvan House, with an admission.

Best time for Walking Tour

Mon. - Fri. .... 10am - 2pm

Cost
Free

Directions

On Chapparal Street, near the Bayfront Arts and Science Park.

What's Fun about Corpus Christi?

INTERNATIONAL KITE MUSEUM

3200 Surfside
Corpus Christi, TX 78403
512-883-7456

Kites, kites, and more kites

Everything you can image having to do with kites you will find here in this small museum.

The history of the kite from the Orient, Europe, and the U.S.; uses of the kite in science and warfare; and "cool" kites in the Kite Shoppe. They have a terrific selection. Give your kites a try outside on the beach.

Absolutely delightful! Great for the whole family!

Hours
Daily . . . . 10am - 5pm

Cost
Free

Directions
Inside the Best Western Sandy Beach Resort Hotel.

What's Fun about Corpus Christi?

KING RANCH
Kingsville, TX 78364
512-592-8055

One of the most interesting tours ever!

The King Ranch is a national historic landmark, the birthplace of the ranching industry, and still a working family business. One of the most famous and largest ranches in the world, 825,000 acres in all, the King Ranch is larger than the state of Rhode Island. Can't say enough about this place, be sure to visit. You will be impressed by the magnitude, the history, and the strong pioneering family that created the Ranch and still runs it today. Their 90-minute guided bus tour beginning at the Ranch Visitor Center is well worth the time and money.

Hours for Tours
Tours begin every hour, on the hour
Mon. - Sat. .... 10am - 3pm
Sun. .... 1pm - 4pm

Cost
(Tour includes a discount to the Museum)
Adults $7
Children $2.50

Directions
From Corpus Christi, take Highway 77 South to Kingsville and go right (east) on King Street. Follow to the King Ranch Entrance.

What's Fun about Corpus Christi?

KING RANCH VISITOR CENTER

Learn about the Ranch's 143-year history on video.

Hours

Mon. - Sat. .... 9am - 4pm
Sun. .... Noon - 4pm

GUIDED NATURE TOURS

The King Ranch also offers guided nature tours, pinpointing wildlife habitats. See an immense population of animals: tropical and migratory birds, white-tailed deer, javelinas, and coyotes. Vary depending on the time of the year and wildlife. Call for more information.

KING RANCH SADDLE SHOP

201 E. Kleberg Avenue
Kingsville, TX 78364
800-282-KING

Famous-brand leather goods

Purchase handmade leather goods with the famous Running W brand at the Saddle Shop located in the historic Ragland Mercantile Company building. Be sure to make this part of your visit to the Ranch.

Directions

From Corpus take Hwy. 77 South to Kingsville and go right (east) on King St., then right on 6th St. Will be on the corner of 6th and Kleberg St's.

KING RANCH MUSEUM
405 N. 6th Street
Kingsville, TX 78363
512-595-1881

Historical items of interest

Housed in a circa-1907 ice factory and power plant, the Museum exhibits interesting historical items pertaining to the King family, including photos from 1940's life on the Ranch, a collection of saddles from around the world, antique carriages and vintage cars.

Hours
Mon. - Sat. .... 10am - 4pm
Sun. .... 1pm - 5pm

Cost
Adults $4
Children ages 12-5 .... $2.50
Children under 5 .... Free

Directions

From Corpus take Hwy 77 South to Kingsville and go right (east) on King St. then right on 6th St. three blocks.

What's Fun about Corpus Christi?

NAVAL STATION INGLESIDE

Ingleside on the Bay
512-776-4204 • 512-776-5939

Bus tour of naval base

The Naval Station at Ingleside is home to more than a dozen U.S. Navy ships and is headquarters for the Navy's mine warfare program. It employs 37,000 active-duty military and 550 civilians.

The bus tour lasts about an hour and makes a loop around the Base, stopping at the waterfront to observe the three classes of ships that port here.

Once a month on Saturday, 1-4pm, one of the more countermeasure ships is open to the public for guided tours. Call for schedule.

Hours for tour

(Check-in for tour at the front gate)
Tuesday 1:30pm

Cost

Free

Directions

From Corpus Christi, take Hwy 181 across the bridge to Portland. Continue on Hwy 35. Exit onto 361 going into Ingleside. Watch for signs. At the 4-way stop, go right on 1069 for 5 miles.

What's Fun about Corpus Christi?

PADRE ISLAND NATIONAL SEASHORE

Park Headquarters
9405 South Padre Island Dr.
Corpus Christi, TX 78418
512-949-8068

National park with beautiful beaches

Padre Island National Seashore is the longest seashore in America. Its undeveloped beaches with white, windswept sand dunes, wild grasslands, tidal flats, and warm waters beckon visitors—as well as 350 species of bird.

Camp at primitive campsites, surf, swim, fish, or hike the 3/4-mile grassland nature trail. Comb the beach for driftwood and seashells (especially good on winter and spring days at low tide).

The visitors center complex houses an observation deck, restrooms, rinse-off showers, changing rooms, a grocery store, and a gift shop.

Hours

Visitors Center
Daily (Summer) .... 9am - 6pm
Park
(Open all the time)

Cost

(Entrance fee is good for 10 days)
Per Car $10

Directions

Located at the end of Park Road 22.

What's Fun about Corpus Christi?

SOUTH TEXAS INSTITUTE FOR THE ARTS

1902 N. Shoreline Blvd.
Corpus Christi, TX 78401
512-980-3500

Community art center, beautifully housed

Permanent and major changing exhibits are housed in this beautiful facility designed by nationally known architect Philip Johnson.

Affiliated with Texas A&M University-Corpus Christi, the Institute's mission is to promote American and regional visual art through exhibitions, collection, and educational opportunities. They do a great job; take time to visit.

Close to the museum are the Water Gardens, with 150 jet fountains. Delightful! Great photo opportunity!

Hours

Closed Monday

Tues.-Sat	10am - 5pm
Sunday	1pm - 5pm

Cost

Adults	$3
Seniors & Military	$2
Children (ages 2-18)	$1
Children (under 2)	Free

Directions

Located in the Bayfront Art and Science Park.

What's Fun about  *Corpus Christi?*

SPORT FISHING IN THE COASTAL BEND AREA

Area piers, jetties, and guides

Whether your preference is deep sea or bay fishing, line casting from a pier or jetty, surf fishing, or fly fishing in the marshes, you'll get hooked on what the Corpus Christi area has to offer.

PIERS AND JETTIES

Bob Hall Pier
On Padre Island, in Padre Balli County Park.

Breakwater Jetty
Near Corpus Christi Bay Marina.

Colepark Pier
In Corpus Christi, off Ocean Drive.

Indian Point
Hwy. 181, between Corpus Christi and Portland.

Nueces Bay Pier
On Corpus Christi Beach, at the Hull Street exit.

Oso Pier
6123 Ocean Drive.

SALTWATER FISHING SPOTS

Listed are the best saltwater fishing spots on the Coastal Bend. The area includes bays and backwater bays around Rockport, Port Aransas, and Corpus Christi.

Aransas Bay

The bays situated behind San Jose Island include the Aransas Bay System: Copano, St. Charles, and South Bays. Excellent fishing in these waters due to the shallow grass flats in the South and Redfish Bays and the oyster reefs in sheltered Capano Bay.

Corpus Christi Bay

Corpus Christi Bay credits good fishing to its shallow shoreline and the fish-attracting reefs in its "back bay" (Nueces Bay).

Upper Laguna Madre

The waters behind Padre Island, the longest barrier island in the Northern Hemisphere, are recognized the worldover for their excellent fishing. This is one of only two hypersaline bays in the world with fish-loving shallow grassy flats.

Baffin Bay

This shallow inlet body of water is famous for its trophy-size speckled trout due to its hypersaline environment.

What's Fun about Corpus Christi?

RECOMMENDED FISHING GUIDES & PIERS

Prepare yourself for some of the best fishing in the country. Below are deep-sea and bay fishing guides and party boats. The fishing guides take 1-6 people fishing in Laguna Madre and Baffin Bays for trophy-size speckled trout and redfish. The party boats are more affordable.

Alta's Star Trek
(party boat-bay fishing) 512-883-5031

Capt. Allen Sifford's "Fish On"
(private guide) 512-939-8787

Capt. Carl Wentrcek Guide Service
(private guide) 800-368-8175 • 512- 937-0868

Capt. Jon Fails
(private guide) 512-949-0133

Capt. Terry Panknin
(private guide)
800-992-8393 • 512-992-8368

Capt. Wallace Kelly
(private guide)
800-388-7311 • 512-939-8045

Captain Clark
(party boats, bay fishing) 512-884-4369

Copeland's Marine
(deep-sea fishing charter)
800-567-5132 • 512-854-1135

What's Fun about  *Corpus Christi?*

Don's Guide Service
(private guide) 512-993-2024

Ingram's Guide Service
(private guide) 512-857-0702 • 800-368-6032

FISHING PIERS

Bob Hall Pier
On Padre Island at Padre Balli Park.
512-949-0999

Breakway Jetty
Near the Corpus Christi Bay Marina.

Cole Park Pier
In Corpus Christi on Ocean Drive.

Indian Point Pier
On Highway 181,
between Corpus Christi and Portland.
512-643-8555

Nueces Bay Pier
On Corpus Christi Beach,
take the Hull Street Exit.

Oso Pier
512-991-9986 • 512-991-3001
At 6124 Ocean Drive.

What's Fun about Corpus Christi?

TEXAS STATE AQUARIUM

P.O. Box 331307 • Corpus Christi, TX 78463
512-881-1200 • 800-477-GULF

Official Aquarium of Texas

This 7.3 acre interpretive center, with indoor and outdoor exhibits, is designed to take you from the shores of the Gulf of Mexico to the depths of its waters. Even the 40-foot acrylic tunnel entrance gives you the feeling you're going underwater.

On-site programs range from dive shows and feeding demonstrations to opportunities to actually touch sharks and rays.

Many of the displays are hands-on and let you see marine life in its natural habitat. Caring about our endangered species, the aquarium teaches us to take special care of our marine and native wildlife. I enjoyed the river otters the most. They will delight any audience just being themselves.

An outstanding attraction that you will want to take your family to see. Plan to take your time to really enjoy what is here. Very educational to say the least.

Hours

Mem Day- Labor Day 'til 6pm /Tues. 'til 8pm
Mon.-Sat. 9am-5pm
Sun. 10am-5pm

Cost

Adults.................................... $8
Children (ages 12-17) $6.75
Children (ages 4-11) $4.50
Children (under 4) .... Free

Directions

Cross Harbor Bridge. Take the first exit to the right.

What's Fun about Corpus Christi?

WORLD OF DISCOVERY

1900 N. Chaparral, Corpus Christi, TX
512-883-2862 • 512-886-4492

Corpus Christi has a first-class museum

Discover how superb the Corpus Christi Museum of Science and History really is. Stop first at the "Seeds of Change" exhibit from the Smithsonian Institute. It details changes wrought in the New World by five "seeds": horses, sugar, corn, potatoes, and disease. Then discover the "Shipwreck" exhibit of three ships wrecked in 1554 on Padre Island.

Next visit life-size replicas of the Nina, Pinta, and Santa Maria, built by Spain to commemorate the 500th anniversary of Christopher Columbus' voyage. Fortunately, Corpus Christi is now their homeport. Brought out of the water for repairs, they sit in a re-creation of a 15th-century shipyard where visitors not only observe them but experience climbing aboard. Guides in period costumes demonstrate knot-tying, 15th-century cooking, and navigational techniques. Great activity for the whole family. Where else could you have an experience like this?

Hours

Daily . . . . 10am - 6pm

Cost

Adults	$8
Senior (60+) & active Military	$6.50
Children (ages 13-17)	$7
Children (ages 5-12)	$4
Children (under 4)	Free

Directions

Located in the Bayfront Arts and Science Park.

What's Fun about  *Corpus Christi?*

USS LEXINGTON

P.O. Box 23076, Corpus Christi, TX 78403
512-888-4873 • 800-523-9539

Tour an aircraft carrier

Commissioned in 1943, this aircraft carrier served longer and set more records than any other carrier in US naval history. The USS Lexington saw World War II action in almost every major sea campaign in the Pacific Theater of Operations, even taking a Kamikaze hit.

Nicknamed "The Blue Ghost" by Japanese radio propagandist Tokyo Rose, the Lexington was reported as having been sunk four different times. Each time the reports proved false.

Tours include the flight deck, engine room and sick bay, the hangar deck, captain and admiral quarters, foc'sle, and the navigation and flag bridges.

Exhibits cover daily activity aboard the aircraft carrier during World War II: mine warfare, antiaircraft guns, American prisoners of war.

Visitors can enjoy the 19 vintage aircraft and a state-of-the-art flight simulation.

Hours

Daily 9am-5pm
Memorial Day to Labor Day - 'til 6pm
Closed Christmas Day

Cost

Adults....................................	$9
Senior (60+) & active Military	$7
Children (ages 4-12)	$4

Directions

Across Harbor Bridge, take the first right.

What's Fun about  *Corpus Christi?*

WATERFRONT ART MARKET & ART GALLERIES

People Street T-Head
512-880-3474

Bimonthly art event

Held the 1st and 3rd Sundays of each month, March - December, at the People Street T-Head, from 10am - 5pm. Open to all artists and crafts.

What's Fun about Corpus Christi?

WATCH FOR THESE ANNUAL EVENTS

South Texas Ranching Heritage Festival
(February)
512-593-2819
Conner Museum, A&M, celebrates
the ranching heritage.

Annual Stage Door Canteen
(February)
512-800-Lady-Lex
Abroad the USS Lexington, recreation of World War II,
USO-type entertainment.

Annual South Texas
Ranching Heritage Festival
(March) - Kingsville
512-593-2819
Ranch craftsmen and artisans sell wares. Featuring
campfire stories, poetry, music, and rodeo. Also,
chuckwagon cookoff and campfire cooking.

Buccaneer Day and Rodeo
(Last week of April into May)
512-882-3242
Commemorates landing of Spanish explorer Alonza
Alvares. Parades, fireworks, carnival.

What's Fun about Corpus Christi?

Ingleside Navy Days
(May)
512-776-2906
Sunset salute to the Armed Forces
with food and activities.

TejanoFest
(May) - Corpus Christi
512- 985-1555

At Texas SkyFestival Park, 6925 Jurica Park. Biggest in Tejano Festivals in South Texas. Features a variety of bands and music all day.

Big Bang Weekend
(July 4-5) - Corpus Christi
512-994-4884

Along the Bay front on Shoreline Drive; a weekend of activities, with music, food, an evening parade before the fireworks at 9pm.

Stars & Stripes
(July 4) - Corpus Christi
888-4873 • 800-Lady Lex

Aboard the USS Lexington, the Corpus Christi Symphony plays the 1812 Overture with cannon fire and fireworks.

Great Texas Birding Classic
888-TX-BIRD • 1-800-678-6232
Guides to the best birding sites on the Texas Coastal Bend. Local community activities.

What's Fun about Corpus Christi?

Bayfest & Folklife Celebration
(End of Sept. - First of Oct.)
512-887-0868
Gaining popularity, began as a Bicentennial event; fireworks, parade, Coast Guard demo.

Annual Texas Jazz Festival
(October) - Corpus Christi
512-883-4500
Along the Bayfront.

Annual King Ranch Hand Breakfast
(November)
512-592-8516
Popular and fun event on the King Ranch.
Serves over 5,000.

La Posada De Kingsville
(December) - Kingsville
512-592-8516
Held the 2nd weekend of December in downtown historic Kingsville. A Christmas festival parade, reenacting Joseph and Mary's search for an inn.

What's Fun about Corpus Christi?

WHAT'S KIDS' STUFF

Botanical Gardens

Playground, picnic area, children's garden, and two easygoing nature trails, one with an observation tower.

Cole Park

On Ocean Drive and Oleander St.
Has a wonderful bay front playground.

International Kite Museum

"The Kite Shoppe" at the museum sells fun kites. Buy the one you like, take it to the beach, and see how it flies.

Kids' Day at Executive Surf Club

309 Water Street • 512-884-7873 - Every Saturday at 1pm, families are invited for free art, crafts, and face painting with a clown and magician. Great time and place to have a birthday party.

Texas State Aquarium

The Island of Steel features dive show and fish feedings the kids will love to see, at 10:30 am, 2:30 pm, and 3:30 pm in the Outdoor Marsh Exhibit. See playful river otters, a touch tank with live stingrays (barbs removed) and sharks, and endangered Kemp's Ridley Sea Turtles. Outside is a marine-theme playground.

World of Discovery

The museum has interesting hand-on exhibits for children and on-going Saturday programs for families. Every Saturday at 1:30 pm, join in a "Treasure Hunt," children's seek-and-find game. See a live alligator. Learn more about dinosaurs.

What's Fun about Corpus Christi?

WHERE TO EAT?

The best places to eat in Corpus Christi

Dentoni's Pizza
415 Williams Street
512-881-9886
Italian food.

GrandView Restaurant and Bar
300 N. Shoreline
512-883-5111

Kiko's Mexican Food Restaurant and Mercado
5514 Everhart
512-991-1211
Mexican food

Landry's Seafood House
600 N. Shoreline (People's Street T-head)
512-882-6666
Floating restaurant offers view of downtown
and shrimp boats.

La Bahia
224 N. Mesquite
512-888-6555
Mexican restaurant

Lighthouse Restaurant and Catering Company

444 N. Shoreline Blvd.
512-883-3982

View of marina and skyline from upper level. Seafood restaurant serving steaks, chicken, pasta dishes, Cajun dishes, and the "catch of the day."

Longhorn Steak and Ale

4307 Avalon St. • 512-992-7731

Rated the "Best of the Best Steaks" in 1993, 1994, and 1995. Grilled chicken, babyback ribs, salads, chicken fried steak, grilled fish, and seafood.

Mamma Mia's

128 N. Mesquite • 512-883-3773
Italian restaurant

Republic of Texas Bar and Grill

900 N. Shoreline Blvd. • 512-886-3515
Steakhouse

The Bar-B-Q Man Restaurant

4931 IH 37 (exit Navigation) • 512-888-4248
Texas style BBQ with brisket, sausage, turkey breast, pork ribs, ham

WaterStreet Seafood Co.

309 N. Water St. • 512-882-8684

Popular quality restaurant with the freshest seafood; have it mesquite charbroiled, spicy, and blackened. Listed blackboard specials, daily. I highly recommend eating here for seafood; try the blackened shrimp.

WHERE TO STAY?

The best places to stay in Corpus Christi
ON THE BAYFRONT

Omni Bayfront Hotel
900 N. Shoreline Blvd.
512-887-1600 • 800-843-6664

Has 474 guest rooms with 28 suites, all bay front views. Within walking distance to the Marina District, Republic of Texas Bar & Grill on premises, health club, heated indoor/outdoor pools.

Omni Marina Hotel
707 N. Shoreline Blvd.
512-882-1700 • 800-843-6664

Has 346 guest rooms with balconies and bay front view, restaurant, indoor/outdoor pools. Minutes from downtown attractions.

Marina Grand Hotel
300 N. Shoreline Blvd.
512-883-5111 • 800-883-5119

Top quality guest rooms, free parking, pool, cable, and the GrandView Restaurant on premises.

Holiday Inn Emerald Beach
1102 S. Shoreline Blvd.
512-883-5731 • 800-HOLIDAY (465-4329)

Has 368 plush guest rooms with bay view, cable, indoor pool, sauna, whirlpool, pingpong, children's playport, fitness center, and 2 restaurants; on the trolley route.

What's Fun about  *Corpus Christi?*

Ramada Inn Bayfront
601 N. Water Street
512-882-8100 • 800-688-0334
Presidential awarded, 3-diamond, 2-star hotel with 200 spacious guest rooms beautifully furnished, cable, work desk, balconies, and many with view of bay.

Harbor Inn Bayfront
411 N. Shoreline
512-884-4815 • 800-538-4238
On the bay, 99 quality guest rooms.

ON PADRE ISLAND:

Holiday Inn Gulf Beach Resort
15202 Windward Dr.
512-949-8041 • 888-949-8041
Only full-service hotel on beach. Sauna, athletic pool, outdoor pool, hot tub, playground, shuffleboard, bike rentals, microwave & refrigerator, restaurant; 15 minutes from Corpus Christi.

Island House Condominiums
15230 Leeward Drive
512-949-8166 • 800-333-8806
Fully furnished kitchens, laundromat, maid and linen service, private balcony with Gulf View, large heated fresh water pool, guset priviledges at Padre Island Country Club.

The Gulfstream Condominiums
14810 Windward Drive
512-949-8061 • 800-542-7368

A full-facility condominium with heated swimming pool and jacuzi, daily maid service, laundry facilities, fully furnioshed kitchens and guest privilegies at the near-by Padre Island Country Club.

El Constante Condominiums
14802 Windward Drive
512-949-7088

This beachfront condominium has a swimming pool and heated jacuzzi, completely equipped kitchens, limited maid service.

ON MUSTANG ISLAND

Port Royal Ocean Resort Condominiums
6317 State Hwy 361
512-749-5011 • 800-242-1034

The condominium is directly on the beach with fully equipped kitchens, washers, dryers, wet bar, stereo, sundeck balconies, whirlpool tub and many more extras. The 500 ft. lagoon swimming pool with 4 hot tubs and the "Twisting Dune" water slide. The Atrium Restaurant offers an incredible gulf view, serving breakfast, lunch, dinner and Sunday Champagne Brunch and room service.

What's Fun about Corpus Christi?

BED AND BREAKFAST

Avalon Boat, Bed & Breakfast
Peoples Street T-Head
512-883-1121

Bay Breeze Bed and Breakfast
201 Louisiana Street
512-882-4123

On the bay in a fine old home with 4 bedroom suites/private bathes. Five minutes from business district.

FKR Bed & Breakfast and Accommodations for Horse & Rider
Farm Road 70, Box 81
Sandia, TX
512-547-2546

Thirty five miles west of Corpus Christi on an old Jersey farm with 3-bedroom guest cottages. Offers gourmet meals served in your cottage, gourmet picnic lunches, horseback riding, canoeing, bird watching, skeet shooting, fishing, hunting, horse riding lessons, and complimentary Continental breakfast.

What's Fun about Corpus Christi?

UNIQUE PLACES TO SHOP

Antiquing Area
4300 South Alameda
Over 60 dealers.
Open 6 days a week from 10am - 6pm.

Moore Plaza
5425 S. Padre Island Drive
HEB Grocery, Target, Old Navy, Hobby Lobby, Builders Square, Office Depot, Pets Mart

Sunrise Mall
S. Padre Island Dr. (at Airline)
512-993-2900
Burlington Coat Factory, Mervyn's, Montgomery Ward, Sears, Stein Mart.

Padre Staples Mall
S. Padre Island Dr. (at Staples)
512-991-5718
Over 130 stores and services. Has a 25-foot double decker, hand-painted carousel.

Water Street Market
Downtown between Water and Williams Street. Bunched together, dont't miss these unique, interesting little shops and fantastic restaurants. The Water Street Seafood Co., Water Street Oyster Bar, Executive Surf Club, and Che Bello ought to top your list of places to eat.

Visit antique stores, art galleries, and shops like Totally Texas, Gifts by the Sea, The Cat House, and The Gold Bug.

SOUTH PADRE AREA

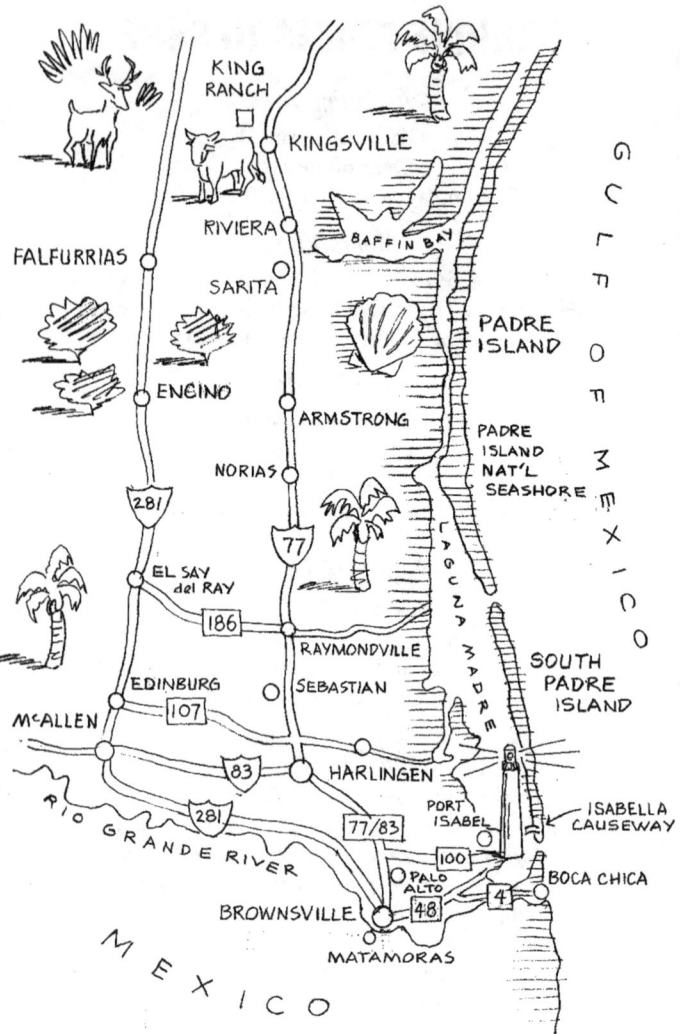

Chapter 7
WHAT'S FUN ABOUT SOUTH PADRE ISLAND?

About South Padre............................ 217

Brownsville

Brownsville Fine Arts Museum.................. 219
Confederate Air Force Museum................. 220
Heritage Trail Tour of Historic Brownsville 221
Historic Brownsville Museum................... 222
Historic Brownsville Trolley Tour............... 223
Gladys Porter Zoo............................ 224
Palo Alto Battlefield National Hictoric Site 225
Palmito Ranch Battlefield 226
Sabal Palm Audubon Center and Sanctuary 227
Santa Ana National Wildlife Refuge 228
Stillman House 229

Harlingen

Battle of Iwo Jima Monument, Museum 230
Laguna Atascosa National Wildlife Refuge 231
Rio Grande Valley Historic Museum & Complex... 232
Texas Air Museum 233

Port Isabel

Port Isabel Historical Museum.................. 234
Port Isabel Lighthouse State Historical Park 235

South Padre Island

Andy Bowie Park............................. 236
Beach Buggies, Bicycles, Jeeps, Roller Blades 237
Bird Watching Sites in the Lower R.G.V. 238

Coastal Studies Laboratory, UT Pan America	241
Diving off South Padre Island	242
Dolphin Watching on Laguna Madre Bay	243
Golfing in the Rio Grande Valley	244
Isla Blanca Park	248
Island Equestrian Center	249
Laguna Madre Nature Trail	250
Sea Turtle, Inc	251
Sea Shelling on South Padre Island	252
Sport Fishing on South Padre Island	253
The Whaling Wall	256
Visiting Matamoras, Mexico	257
Watch for these Annual Events	259
Watersport Rentals	261
What's Kids' Stuff?	263
Where to Eat?	265
Where to Stay?	268
Unique Places to Shop	271

What's Fun about South Padre Island?

South Padre Island

South Padre Island—Texas' version of Waikiki or Malibu. The best beaches, the warmest year-round climate, and the most diversity in activities on the Texas Coast.

This barrier island on the southernmost tip of Texas, with gorgeous white beaches and swaying palm trees, is 34 miles long and only a half mile at its widest point. The climate makes it a haven for Winter Texans, Spring Breakers, and family vacationers.

Tourism is South Padre's only industry, with five distinct tourist seasons. Summertime, of course, is the peak season requiring vacation plans to be made well in advance. A prime time to visit is from Labor Day until Thanksgiving, when the crowds have gone, temperatures are pleasant, and fishing is excellent. You'll also find the best lodging rates in December, January, and February, along with an influx of folks wanting to escape the cold. Then comes an explosion of activity with Spring Breakers and Mexican tourists that lasts through April. After that, there is a very brief season until mid-May when it's quiet again.

Only 30 miles from Matamoros, one of Mexico's nicest border towns, South Padre can give an international flavor to your vacation. Guided bus tours leave the island for Mexico daily. Or simply park and walk across the border to where people are friendly, shopping is a bargain, and the food is safe.

The natives claim their shrimp tastes the best. Arguing would be difficult, since they serve the freshest shrimp possible. While you are there, try one of their seafood restaurants with a fantastic view of Laguna Madre.

What's Fun about South Padre Island?

Not only will you find great restaurants, swanky condos, and fun attractions, there is room to explore nature. An abundance of migratory birds make this their winter home. Bird watching has become popular, as well as fishing, shelling, and crabbing. Be sure to visit the Laguna Atascosa National Wildlife Refuge across the Laguna Madre bay.

This chapter includes neighboring areas such as Brownsville, Harlingen, and Port Isabel. Some of the best Mexican food I ate was in Brownsville.

A word of warning! The Queen Isabella Causeway, the longest bridge in Texas, is the only way to drive onto South Padre Island. Policemen in Port Isabel eagerly hand out traffic tickets to unsuspecting tourists who break the traffic laws in any way. I got a ticket for not wearing my seat belt.

Drive carefully and safely. Hope you have as much fun as I did.

How many miles from South Padre to
Austin	339
Brownsville	48
Dallas	531
El Paso	815
Houston	366
Mexico City	688
San Antonio	286

What's Fun about South Padre Island?

BROWNSVILLE FINE ARTS MUSEUM WILLIAM NEALE HOUSE

230 Neale Dr.
Brownsville TX 78520
956-542-0941

A fine arts museum surrounded with history

Built in 1834 then moved to its present location in 1950, the Neale House is the oldest wood-framed house in Brownsville. William Neale served as mayor and established the stagecoach lines between Matamoros and Bagdad, Mexico, Brownsville, and Port Isabel.

Outside you will see the original gazebo and bandstand from Fort Brown.

The museum contains art exhibits, galleries, and a studio. Famous artists such as Chagall, Daumier, Samualson, and Whistler have their works permanently on display at this museum, plus works of many local artists.

Hours

Open year around

Mon – Fri .... 9:30am – 3pm
Sunday .... 1pm - 5pm

Cost

Free - Donations Accepted

Directions

Take State Hwy 48 towards Brownsville (south). State Hwy 48 becomes the International Boulevard. Exit Elizabeth Street going left and then right on Porter Drive. Porter Drive becomes Neale Street.

What's Fun about South Padre Island?

CONFEDERATE AIR FORCE MUSEUM RIO GRANDE VALLEY WING

955 Minnesota
Brownsville, TX 78520
956-541-8585

See vintage aircraft in a class of its own

The fifteen vintage aircraft housed in this museum can still fly! Besides having historical aircraft from World War II and the Korean War, you will also see fascinating memorabilia and artifacts from that era.

Watch the video presentation and visit the gift shop. The Fiesta Air Show is a popular annual event, held in early March.

Hours

Monday – Saturday .... 9am – 4pm

Cost

Adults $5
Senior $4
Students $3
Children under 12 .... Free

Directions

At the Brownsville/South Padre Island Airport

What's Fun about South Padre Island?

HERITAGE TRAIL TOUR OF HISTORIC BROWNSVILLE

Brownsville Convention & Visitors Bureau
650 FM 802
Brownsville, TX. 78520
956-546-3721•800-626-2639

Self-guided walking tours of Brownsville's historical sites

Get acquainted with the area's rich history when you explore these historical sites of Brownsville. Take a series of nine short self-guided walking tours past some of Brownsville's most important historical homes and buildings. Each segment takes approximatly 10 to 20 minutes. Official markers post the beginning of each trail site.

Begin your tour at the Historic Brownsville Museum, the original townsite. The original townsite, near downtown Brownsville, brags of homes, businesses, restaurants, and a cathedral from the mid-1800's. Take your time and have fun.

Maps for this activity can be purchased at the Brownsville Convention and Visitors Bureau. Ask for the "Guide to Historic Brownsville."

Hours

Mon. - Sat. .... 8am - 5pm
Sun. .... 9am - 4 pm

Cost

Guide booklet $2

Directions

At the corner of FM 802 and Highway 77/83.

What's Fun about South Padre Island?

HISTORIC BROWNSVILLE MUSEUM

641 E. Madison Street
Brownsville, TX 78520
956-548-1313

Brownsville's got great history

The old Southern Pacific Railroad Depot built in 1928 in the Spanish Colonial Revivalist Style houses the Historic Brownville Museum.

You will find many interesting historical photographs, artifacts, and documents, particularly about the area's military history.

The museum is in the original townsite of Brownsville, and many of the homes, businesses, restaurants, and the cathedral date back to the mid-1800's.

Hours

(Closed Sundays)

Mon. - Fri. .... 10am - 4:30pm
Saturday .... 10am - 1pm

Cost

Adults $2
Students .... $.50

Directions

At East 6th and Madison Streets.

What's Fun about South Padre Island?

HISTORIC BROWNSVILLE TROLLEY TOUR

Brownsville Convention & Visitors Bureau
956-546-3721 • 800-626-2639

A narrated trolley ride that originates from the Brownsville Convention & Visitors Bureau Information Center offers a great tour of the city that the whole family will enjoy.

Enjoy riding in a turn-of-the-century trolley that is comfortable, clean, and air-conditioned. Guides are knowledgeable and friendly. The trolley is also handicapped accessible.

You will get a taste of Brownsville's rich heritage and a glimpse of her major attractions, including the world-class Port of Brownsville.

Make your reservations 24 hours in advance. Tours can be customized for your group.

Hours

Port of Brownsville
Monday	10am - 1pm

Historic Museum
Tues., Thurs., & Fri.	10am
Wed. & Sat.	1pm

Stillman House
Wed. & Sat.	10am
Tues., Thurs., & Fri.	1pm

Cost

Adults	$7
Children (ages 12 & under)	$3.50

Directions

At the corner of FM 802 and Highway 77/83

What's Fun about South Padre Island?

GLADYS PORTER ZOO

500 Ringgold Street
Brownsville, TX 78520
Office 956-546-7187
Recording 956-546-2177

A very special zoo in Brownsville

Opening in 1971, this multi-million dollar, 31-acre facility was a dream come true for Gladys Porter, daughter of the 1st President of the J.C. Penney Company.

Visit one of the best zoos in our nation. See attractive open-air habitats, with beautiful award-winning landscaping, designed with the animals and visitors in mind. The Gladys Porter Zoo is concerned with the survival of endangered species and includes some that are very rare. It is known for successfully breeding many of them.

See animals from all over the world: the Tropical American section with jaguars and huge tortoises, the Indo-Australian section with wallabies and kangaroos, the Asian section with the typical zoo animals like African elephants, zebras and pileated gibbons. Be sure to take the kids to the children's zoo and nursery.

Hours

Daily . . . . 9am – 5pm
(with extended summer hours)

Cost

Adults $6.00
Children (ages 13-2) $3.00
Children (under 2) . . . . Free

Directions

At Ringgold and Sixth Streets.

What's Fun about South Padre Island?

PALO ALTO BATTLEFIELD NATIONAL HISTORIC SITE

Visitor Center
1623 Central Blvd.
Brownsville, TX
956-541-2785

Historical Site and Visitor Center

Learn what took place at this battle between the United States and Mexico. On May 8, 1846, the battle began as General Zachary Taylor's men marched onto the Palo Alto prairie and the Mexican cannons opened fire. The Mexican Army was overwhelmed and defeated, finally liberating Fort Texas. With this victory, the US claimed disputed lands north of the Rio Grande.

President Bush signed authorization for a Battlefield National Historical Site June 23, 1993. He also mandated that each country's perspective of the war be represented. The exhibits are temporarily housed at this address, including interesting artifacts, historical information, and a video program about this battle. Be sure to visit.

Hours

Monday – Friday .... 8am – 5pm

Cost

Free

Directions

North of Brownsville, at the intersection of FM 1847 and FM 511. The exhibits are on the 2nd floor of the International Bank of Commerce Building at 1623 Central Boulevard.

PALMITO RANCH BATTLEFIELD

Last battle of the Civil War

See where the last battle of the Civil War was fought, five weeks after General Lee surrendered in Appomattox.

On May 12 and 13, 1865, the Confederates, commanded by Colonel John S. Ford captured the federal forces in a winning encounter, but only when their prisoners told them did they learn they had already lost the war.

See the historical marker pinpointing the site of this last great battle. (No visitor center)

Hours
Sunrise to sunset

Cost
Free

Directions
On Texas State Highway 4,
located 8 miles east of Brownsville.

What's Fun about South Padre Island?

SABAL PALM AUDUBON CENTER AND SANCTUARY

P.O. Box 5052 (On FM 1419)
Brownsville, TX 78523
956-541-8034

One-of-a-kind wildlife sanctuary

See the largest, best-preserved grove of native Texas Sabal Palm that once grew abundantly along the banks of the Rio Grande. This 527-acre wildlife preserve is owned and operated by the National Audubon Society. Few of these trees exist any where else in the United States.

Three 1/2-mile nature trails leave from the visitor center, wander through the Sabal Palm grove and on down to the Rio Grande. The endangered jaguarundi (a rare cat) is believed to exist within the sanctuary, along with other interesting wildlife.

The visitor center offers school tours, activities, presentations, and workshops. Call for information.

Visitors Center Hours

Oct. - May (Tues. - Sun.) .... 9am - 5pm
June - Sept. (Sat. - Sun.) .... 9am - 5pm

Cost

Adults $3
Students $2
National Audobon Members $2
Children (ages 6 & under) $1
Special Tours/ per person $5

Directions

From South Padre Island, take Hwy 48 to FM 511, then east to FM 1419. Turn right and go half a mile to the entrance on the left.

What's Fun about South Padre Island?

SANTA ANNA NATIONAL WILDLIFE REFUGE

Route 2 Box 202 A
Alamo, TX 78516
956-787-3079

Wildlife refuge with tram tours

Take a guided tram tour with a naturalist through the subtropical thorn-forest, a natural habitat for much of South Texas wildlife. Part of the US Fish and Wildlife Service's program. This area also has hiking trails, a driving tour, a visitor center, and a gift shop.

The tram operates Thursday through Monday.

Hours
Sunrise to Sunset

Visitor Center
Daily .... 9am – 4:30pm

Cost
Adult $3
Children (under 12) $1

Directions
Located 7 miles south of Alamo, Texas
on US Highway 281 and FM 907.

What's Fun about South Padre Island?

STILLMAN HOUSE

1305 E. Washington Street
Brownsville, TX 78520
956-542-3929

Learn about this grand old house

Visit this old 1850's home, the one-time residence of the founder of Brownsville, Charles Stillman. Now maintained by the Brownsville Historical Society.

This fantastic old house, with its wonderful artifacts, heirlooms, and possessions, makes history come alive.

The gift shop offers historical books, coins, and pictures for sale. A must-see when exploring Brownsville.

In Brownsville for the holidays? See the house beautifully decorated with teddy bears. This is also part of the Trolley Tours, a recommended way to see this historical site.

Hours

Mon – Fri .... 10am – Noon & 2pm – 5pm
Sunday .... 3pm – 5 pm

Cost

Adults $2
Children .... $.50

Directions

On 13th and Washington Streets.

What's Fun about South Padre Island?

BATTLE OF IWO JIMA MOMUMENT, MUSEUM, AND GIFT SHOP

320 Iwo Jima Blvd.
Harlingen, TX
800-365-6006 • 956-423-6006

Filled with memorabilia and artifacts from the bloodiest and costliest battle in Marine Corps history, the museum honors the men who fought on Iwo Jima.

See photos, flags, and relics from the Korean, Vietnam, and Persian Gulf Wars and the Iwo Jima Hall of Fame. Watch the video on the "The Battle for Iwo Jima," shown every 30 minutes with actual combat footage.

See the famous original gypsum-based sculpture depicting the raising of the US flag over Iwo Jima during World War II. It was created from a Pulitzer Prize winning news photo. This monument was used to cast the famous bronze monument at the Marine Corps Memorial in Arlington, Virginia.

Hours

Monday – Saturday	10am – 4pm
Sunday	1pm – 4pm

Cost

Free (Donations are appreciated)

Directions

In Harlingen, on the Marine Military Academy Campus next to the Valley International Airport.

What's Fun about South Padre Island?

LAGUNA ATASCOSA NATIONAL WILDLIFE REFUGE

P.O. Box 450
Rio Hondo, TX 78583
956-748-3608

Popular with birdwatchers, this area is known to have many endangered species such as the brown pelican and the ocelot. (Here you will see some of the only ocelots left in our country).

This particular coastal wetland was spared the development of the 1900's and made part of the wildlife refuge system in 1946.

The Bayside Drive auto tour takes you on a 15-mile loop with numerous places for taking pictures and observing. Be sure to take this drive.

Hours

Refuge open year-round sunrise to sunset

Visitor Center
October through April

Daily .... 10am – 4pm
May Weekends .... 10am – 4pm

Cost

Per vehicle $2

Directions

From South Padre Island, take Highway 100, exit right on FM 510 at Laguna Vista. Continue 5.4 miles to the Cameron County Airport road. Take a right and continue approximately 7 miles to the Visitor Center.

What's Fun about South Padre Island?

RIO GRANDE VALLEY HISTORICAL MUSEUM & COMPLEX

Boxwood at Raintree
Harlingen, TX 78550
956-430-8500

Museum about the Rio Grande Valley

Come away with a better understanding of the history of the Rio Grande Valley.

Within the complex you will find such exhibits as the "New Museum," the "Historical Museum," an "1905 home," a "Paso Real Stage Coach Inn," and "Harlingen's Hospital Museum."

Nice facility and place to go. Make a reservation to take a tour.

Hours

Closed Monday and Tuesday
Wednesday – Saturday .... 10am – 4pm
Sunday .... 1pm – 5pm

Cost

Free (Donations are appreciated)

Directions

At Boxwood and Raintree Street in Harlingen, at the Valley International Airport Complex.

What's Fun about South Padre Island?

TEXAS AIR MUSEUM
P.O. Box 70
Rio Hondo, TX 78583
956-748-2112

Having Focke-Wulf FW-190's

Founded in 1985, this museum features aircraft with a history in Texas, Mexico, World War I, Korea, Vietnam, and Agricultural Aviation. The focus is on aviation history that is less known. The museum houses over 50 aircraft, having a full, on-site restoration facility.

Popular with tourists from all over the world, as well as local school groups. Volunteers eagerly answer questions. Plan to spend some time. A great family activity.

Hours

Monday – Saturday .... 9am - 4 pm
Sunday .... Noon - 4 pm

Cost

Adults $4
Children (ages 12 - 16) $2
Children (under 12) $1

Directions

On FM 106, one mile east of Rio Hondo or
7 miles east of Harlingen.

What's Fun about South Padre Island?

PORT ISABEL HISTORICAL MUSEUM

317 East Railroad
Port Isabel, TX 78578
956-943-7602

Port Isabel has a great historical museum

History is well explained in this unique little museum, housed in an old general store that once sold everything from food to fishing supplies.

Learn about the Indians that inhabited South Padre Island, the Spanish galleons that roamed the Gulf, and events of the Civil and Mexican Wars.

See a short video on the history of Port Isabel, the one-time "Shrimp Capital of the World" in the 1950's and 1960's.

Recently opening to the public, this new museum houses interesting artifacts and photographs. Educational and Interesting.

Hours

Closed Monday and Tuesday
Wed. – Sat. .... 10am – 4pm
Sunday .... 1pm – 4pm

Cost

Adults $1
Children (under 12) .... $.50

Directions

Crossing over the causeway, watch for the museum sign between lanes of opposing traffic. (At the light, take a left, and watch for museum.)

What's Fun about South Padre Island?

PORT ISABEL LIGHTHOUSE STATE HISTORICAL PARK

421 East Queen Isabella Blvd.
Port Isabel, TX 78578
800-527-6102 • 956-943-2262

An 1852 lighthouse that is open to the public

Constructed in 1852 at the request of several sea captains who feared navigating along the shallow Texas coastline, the Port Isabel Lighthouse is the oldest one in Texas. This sixty-foot brick lighthouse is the only lighthouse on the coast open to the public. Be sure to visit.

Take in the panoramic view of the Queen Isabella Causeway and the Laguna Madre Bay as you climb to the top. (This is becoming a popular place to exchange wedding vows.)

Below, the visitor center resembles the original beeper's cottage and houses a great little museum about lighthouses.

The lighthouse will be closed in 1998 for remodeling; call ahead before going.

Hours

Wednesday – Sunday .... 10am - 4pm

Cost

Adult $2
Children (under 12) $1
Children (under 6) .... Free

Directions

Port Isabel on State Highway 100,
at the foot of the causeway.

What's Fun about South Padre Island?

ANDY BOWIE PARK
956-761-2639

County park with family beach and activities

This popular beach is free of vehicles and includes lots of amenities such as picnic pavilions, boogie board and beach umbrella rentals, barbecue grills, concession stands, and a children's playground.

Hours
Daily .... 7:30am - Sunset

Cost
Per vehicle $3

Directions
Located north of the city limits.

What's Fun about South Padre Island?

BEACH BUGGIES, BICYCLES, JEEPS, ROLLER BLADES, SURREYS, AND MORE!

If you prefer your beach vacation on wheels, here are some places to rent them.

Bikini Rover Rentals
1515B Padre Blvd.
956-761-5440
Bikini Rover 2000 (Electric Cars)

Fun Sports
1817 Padre Blvd.
956-761-6182
Beach buggies.

Padre Activity Rentals
1809 Padre Blvd. (Palmetto Plaza)
956-761-1569
4x4's, bikes, and tricycles.

Uncle Buggies
1612 Padre Blvd.
956-761-6162
Beach buggies, beach bicycles, mountain bikes, quadricycles, surreys, roller blades, waverunners.

What's Fun about South Padre Island?

BIRD WATCHING SITES
LOWER RIO GRANDE VALLEY
A Birders' Paradise

Bird watching in the lower Rio Grande Valley is popular for a variety of reasons: Texas is the number one bird watching destination in the US. The Rio Grande Valley is one of the top bird watching destination in Texas. Hundreds of species are found in this area. Many are unique to the Valley.

Laguna Madre Nature Trail
7355 Padre Blvd.

Next to the South Padre Island Convention Centre and always open to the public. Offers a 1500-foot boardwalk overlooking 4 acres of wetlands.

Laguna Atascosa National Wildlife Refuge
P.O. Box 450
Rio Hondo, TX 78583
956-748-3607

Hiking trails, auto tours, visitors center, and bird watching tours. Look for the endangered brown pelicans among other birds such as the redhead ducks, snow geese, sandhill cranes, white-tailed hawks, grebes, gannets, anhingas, frigatebirds, bitterns, herons, ibises, flamingos, swans, geese, American vultures, kites, eagles, hawks.

What's Fun about South Padre Island?

Bentsen Rio Grande Valley State Park
P.O. Box 988
Mission, TX 78572
956-585-1107

On the Rio Grande. Visitor center, hiking trails, tour roads, gift shop, picnic area, fishing, and camping. Take 77 North and 83 West to Mission, then take FM 2062 South to the Park.

Boca Chica Wetlands & Beaches

An undeveloped beach east of Brownsville via Texas Highway 4. No facilities. Home to migrating birds like the roseate spoonbill and white Ibis.

Gladys Porter Zoo
500 Ringgold
Brownsville, TX 78520
956-546-7187

Birding trails, tram tours, classes, and visitor information. Look for these birds: green-backed herons, kiskadee flycatchers and common moorhens. At Ringgold and Sixth Street in Brownsville.

Sabal Palm Grove Sanctuary
P.O. Box 5052
Brownsville, TX 78523
956-541-8034

Visitor center with trails wandering to the Rio Grande. Good place to see green jays, buff-bellied hummingbirds, and tropical parulas. On FM 1419.

What's Fun about  *South Padre Island?*

Santa Anna National Wildlife Refuge
Route 2 Box 202A
Alamo, TX 78516
956-787-3079

Hiking trails, auto tours, and visitor center. See chachalaca, green kingfisher, hook-billed Kite and least grebe. On US 281 and FM 907, 7 miles south of Alamo, Texas.

Valley Nature Center
301 S. Border Avenue
Weslaco, TX 78596
956-969-2475

Visitor center, trails, picnic areas, and gift shop.

What's Fun about South Padre Island?

PAN AMERICAN
COASTAL STUDIES LABORATORY
UNIVERSITY OF TEXAS

Isla Blanca Park
South Padre Island
956-761-2644

Marine studies open to the public

Centering on sea-life indigenous to the area, this facility's purpose is to education the public as well as do research.

See twelve small tanks displaying native sea life (including rays and seahorses), a great seashell collection with interesting exhibits for kids to see, and nature films shown continuously throughout the day. Come away with a better understanding of the interrelationships that govern the structure and function of our entire coastal ecosystem. A fun activity for the whole family.

Hours
Closed Saturday
Sunday – Friday . . . . 1:30pm – 4:30pm

Cost
Free (Donations appreciated)
Although the laboratory is free to the public, there is a $4 entry fee into Isla Blanca Park.

Directions
Inside Isla Blanca Park, at the south end of South Padre Island.

What's Fun about South Padre Island?

DIVING OFF SOUTH PADRE ISLAND

Some of the best diving in the state.

South Padre Island features some of the best diving in the state. With clear water only a few miles from shore, this area is fast becoming a diving resort. Divers from Mexico, San Antonio, Dallas, and Houston converge to this area with serious diving in mind.

Sunken ships, an old tug boat, a Spanish galleon, and oil rigs are just a part of the underwater park that has been created for divers. Only 7 miles offshore, the Port Isabel / South Padre Island Artificial Reef offers challenges for all levels of diving skills and is home to a great variety of sea life. The Liberty Ships, three surplus ships from World War II, sunk in 100 feet of water, beckon the best of divers.

Listed are some outfits to contact if you are interested diving:

American Diving
1807 Padre Blvd.
956-761-2030

Ocean Quest Dive Center
5009 Padre Blvd.
956-761-5003

What's Fun about South Padre Island?

DOLPHIN WATCHING ON THE LAGUNA MADRE BAY

Dolphin watching in the Laguna Madre is a popular tourist activity. One of these narrated guided bay cruises will take you to some of the best places for sightseeing dolphin and other interesting attractions.

Toward the end of the tour, a small net is cast out behind the boat and the contents gathered are emptied into a large trough. Passengers get a close-up view of marine life in the bay. See starfish, seahorses, hermit crabs, jellyfish, sting-ray, or whatever comes aboard. Educational as well as entertaining and a great activity for the family.

American Diving
Sea Ranch Marina
956-761-2030
Dolphin watching, nature, sunset and moonlight cruises.

Breakaway Cruises
Sea Ranch Marina
956-761-2212
Dolphin watches, fireworks cruises, Eco tours, sunset cruises and a Texas Barbecue Cruise.

What's Fun about South Padre Island?

GOLFING IN THE RIO GRANDE VALLEY

Golfer's paradise

The temperate climate of the region creates favorable conditions for year-round golfing. If golfing is your bag, take advantage of the opportunities afforded here. The Rio Grande Valley offers a number of courses with greens fees at a bargain.

Valley Inn & Country Club

FM 802 & McAllen
Brownsville, TX
956-548-9199

Features 18-hole, par-70 golf course measuring 6538 yards and an executive 9-hole, par-3 course. Located south of FM 802, between US Highway 77-83 and US Highway 281.

Greens Fees

9 holes	$11.00
18 holes	$16.50
Cart fee	$18.00 /2 people - 18 holes
Cart fee	$10.00 /2 people - 9 holes

Cottonwood Creek Golf Course

1001 S. Ed Carey Dr.
Harlingen, TX
956-428-0766

An executive 9-hole, par-3 golf course measuring 2100 yards. It is one of the finest courses in the Rio Grande Valley.

Greens Fees

9 holes	$5.41
Cart Fee	$6

What's Fun about South Padre Island?

Whispering Winds Golf & Learning Center
2524 W. Spur 54
Harlingen, TX
956-423-2010

A 9 hole, par-3 course measuring 1306 yards. Has a lighted driving range.

Greens Fees
9 holes	$5
18 holes	$8
Cart fee	$5/person/9 holes

Harlingen Country Club
5500 El Camino Real
Harlingen, TX
956-412-4110

A private 18 hole, par-72 championship golf course measuring 6541 yards.

Reciprocal fees
Monday – Friday	$61.13
Saturday & Sunday	$71.86
Cart fee	$12/person/18-holes

Tony Country Club
Harlingen, TX
956-430-6685

This course is ½ mile south of "M" Street in Harlingen and is a 27-hole course measuring 6320 yards. The first 18 holes are par 71 and have a U.S.G.A. rating of 69.1. Pro shop and driving range.

	Greens Fees	Cart Fees
9 holes	$9	$5
18 holes	$11	$9

What's Fun about South Padre Island?

Treasure Hills Country Club
Off Treasure Hills Blvd. on Augusta
956-428-0351

Unique to the Rio Grande Valley, an 18-hole, par-72 course measuring 6960 yards from the champion tee. Designed by Robert Treat Jones. Closed Mondays.

Greens Fees
Tuesday – Friday $21.65
Saturday – Sunday $21.65

Brownsville Golf and Recreation Center
956-541-2582

An 18-hole golf course, par 70 with course yardage of 6049. Thirteen of the 18 holes are water holes. It is on the north side of FM 802, between US Highway 77/83 and FM 1847.

Fort Brown Municipal Golf Course
300 River Levee Drive
Brownsville, TX
956-542-0394

An 18-hole course, par 72 with course yardage of 6072. It is in the historic Fort Brown area. Take Elizabeth Street, east of International Blvd.

Outdoor Resorts/South Padre Jim Paul Golf Course

900 S. Garcia
Port Isabel, TX
956-943-7520

Advertised as one of the most difficult 18-hole par-3 courses you'll ever play.
Greens fee $8

Turn left at the 1st intersection coming off the causeway into Port Isabel. Cross the swing bridge on South Garcia Street.

Rancho Viejo Country Club

1 Rancho Viejo Dr.
Rancho Viejo, TX
800-531-7400
956-350-4000 x620

Has two 18-hole courses: "El Angel" measuring 6518 yards, rating of 71.5; "El Diablo" measuring 6847 yards, rating of 73.7. Full golf practice facilities.
Greens fees $40
Cart fees $12

South Padre Island Golf Club

1 Gulfhouse Road
Laguna Vista, TX
956-943-5678

18-hole full golf facility

Greens fees (includes cart)	Mon. - Thurs. (to 1pm)	$50
	Fri. - Sun. (to 1pm)	$55
	1pm - 4pm	$29
	after 4pm	$25

What's Fun about South Padre Island?

ISLA BLANCA PARK

Padre Blvd.
956-761-5493

Popular beach offering something for everyone

The most popular beach on South Padre Island. Located on the southernmost tip, this park offers something for everyone. You'll find RV camping, pavilions for day use, jetty fishing, surfing, windsurfing, fishermen, showers, and concession stands serving good burgers, tacos, and sodas.

The park includes the Coastal Studies Laboratory with a visitor center open and free to the public. The aquariums of native sea life and collection of specimens make for a fun afternoon. The park is just south of Jeremiah's, a small, well-run amusement park with waterslides and arcades.

The park is adjacent to the Sea Ranch Restaurant, one of the best seafood restaurants on the island, a marina with fishing charters, and bay cruises to see the dolphins. You will find plenty of activities and fun here.

Depending on the time of year, this beach can be very crowded. A favorite with Spring Breakers, Winter Texans, and families.

Hours
Daily .... 8am – 8:30pm

Cost
Per Vehicle $4

Directions
On the southernmost tip of South Padre Island, south of the causeway.

What's Fun about South Padre Island?

ISLAND EQUESTRIAN CENTER

P.O. Box 3633
South Padre Island, TX 78597
956-761-4677 • 800-761-4677

Horseback riding on the beach

This outfit caters to tourists with little or no experience riding a horse and includes pony rides for small children. Expert riders welcome.

Offers four beach rides daily. Early morning and sunset rides are most enjoyable in the summertime. Group discounts are available. (All-wheel drive beach excursions also available.)

Wear comfortable casual clothing, shoes, and a hat. Bring along the bug repellent and sunscreen. Don't forget the camera. Call at least one hour in advance for reservations.

Hours

Hours vary .... call for times.

Cost (per person)

$25-35 (discounts for children available)

Directions

One mile north of the Convention Centre.

What's Fun about South Padre Island?

LAGUNA MADRE NATURE TRAIL

South Padre Convention Centre
7355 Padre Blvd.

Nature trail for seeing wildlife and beautiful sunsets

The 1500-foot boardwalk overlooks four acres of wetlands and tidal flats that beckon a variety of birds and wildlife; includes interpretive signs with interesting facts about the dune ecosystem and the species of birds you are likely to see.

This is one of the best places to view a spectacular sunset on South Padre Island.

The nature trial begins at the South Padre Island Convention Centre and the 160-foot Whaling Wall. The walkway is always open to the public and is a great family activity, weather permitting.

Wear comfortable shoes, bring the camera and bug repellent. Binoculars come in handy. Watch the little ones.

Hours
Open any time to the public

Cost
Free

Directions
Located next to the South Padre Convention Centre, north of town.

What's Fun about South Padre Island?

SEA TURTLE, INC.
5805 Gulf Blvd.
956-761-2544

Learn about our endangered sea turtles

You may have heard of Ila Loetscher, known throughout the country as the Turtle Lady. Now in her 90's, she single-handedly brought the plight of the endangered Kemp's Ridley Sea Turtle to the public's attention through her television appearances, including the Johnny Carson show.

Now retired in Brownsville, Ms. Loetscher donates her house on South Padre Island to the cause of protecting these creatures. Her staff educates and delights many visitors with shows featuring her cast of endangered and injured turtles.

Here is a rare opportunity to see live sea turtles. You'll leave with a greater appreciation for these creatures and Ila Loetscher's efforts.

A popular program; arrive early. Great for the whole family.

Hours
Tuesday 10am
Saturday 10am

Cost
Per person .... $2.00 donation required

Directions
In a bluish-green house
on the north side of town.

What's Fun about South Padre Island?

SEA SHELLING ON SOUTH PADRE ISLAND

Where to comb the beaches

Shelling on South Padre Island can be fun. You'll find shells with an infinite variety of shapes, colors, and sizes, which will please any collector from the toddler on up.

The best time for shelling is during low tide (in January and February). Best places to go shelling are on Boca Chica Beach, on the bayside of the island and Port Isabel, and beaches north of South Padre Island's city limits.

Boca Chica Beach is an undeveloped beach facing the Gulf, south of Padre Island. The beach is 22 miles long and can be reached by way of Texas 4, east of Brownsville.

If you love seashells, Shell Kingdom may have everything you're looking for. Located a short distance from Port Isabel in Laguna Heights on Texas 100.

What's Fun about South Padre Island?

SPORT FISHING SOUTH PADRE ISLAND

The South Padre Island area offers some of the finest fishing in Texas. There are many different types of fishing and services to choose from. Listed are some popular types of fishing, charter services and fishing piers.

Different types of fishing

Freshwater Fishing-Bass, Crappie, and other fish can be caught year-round from the banks of the Rio Grande's old riverbed, canals, and lakes around Brownsville.

Channel Fishing-from the Brownsville Ship Channel's banks, for trout, croaker, bass, drum.

Pier and Jetty Fishing-there are two lighted fishing piers over Laguna Madre, open 24 hours daily and the jetty in Isla Blanca Park, where fishing can be excellent.

Private Bay Charters-Fish in an 18-foot to 24-foot boat (with a guide), for Speckled Trout, Redfish, Flounder, Snook, Black Drum in the shallow flats of Laguna Madre bay. Offers five-hour fishing trips at $200 for 1 to 2 people.

Private Deep Sea Charters-Fish with a guide for Blue Marlin, White Marlin, Sailfish, Mahi Mahi, Kingfish, Spanish Mackerel, Wahoo, Ling, Bonita, Yellow and Blackfin Tuna. Half-day rates are around $350/person and $800 to $1000/person for a full day.

Party Boats for Bay Fishing-Fish in the bay on boats with large deck. Four-hour trips are $14/person.

Party Boats for Deep-Sea Fishing—Bottom fish (with a group) for red snapper, grouper, amberjack, ling, and shark. Prices start at $60 for 1/2 day of fishing. Full day trips available.

What's Fun about South Padre Island?

FISHING CHARTER SERVICES

These large outfits can provide the type of charter fishing you'd want.

Fisherman's Wharf
211 West Swordfish, South Padre Island, TX
800-752-9889
956-761-7818

Jim's Pier
209 W. Whiting-Bayside at 2nd light
South Padre Island, TX
956-761-2865

Sea Ranch Fishing Pier
1 Padre Blvd.—Right off the Causeway.
956-761-4665

R & R Charter Service
913 Trout Street
Port Isabel, TX
956-943-6311

FISHING PIERS

The Fishing Pier
501 Maxan Street
Port Isabel, TX
956-943-7437

The longest, lighted fishing pier on the Laguna Madre. Open daily, 24 hours-weather permitting. Rents tackle, sells bait, drinks and snacks. Located at the base of the Causeway in Port Isabel. Fish for sand trout, flounder, speckled trout, and whiting.

Sea Ranch Fishing Pier
1 Padre Blvd.
South Padre Island, TX
956-761-4665

At the foot of the Causeway. Open 24 hours a day, weather permitting. With bait, tackle, fishing licenses, ice, snacks, clean restrooms and a playground. Offers charter boat service.

What's Fun about South Padre Island?

THE WHALING WALL

South Padre Island Convention Centre
7355 Padre Blvd.

Artist honors South Padre Island

A famous environmental artist, Wyland, has a goal to paint 100 walls throughout the country. He has completed one at the South Padre Island Convention Centre.

It is an honor to South Padre Island to have the 53rd of its kind, depicting the beauty of our whales and other marine life. The artist hopes to raise our public awareness of our environment and help save endangered whales.

A fun family activity that takes a few moments and something you can't miss seeing. Simply view this magnificent painting from your car or better yet, make it part of your experience on the Laguna Madre Nature Trail.

This great accomplishment will bring you joy, appreciation, and a understanding for purpose.

Hours
Open to the public any time

Cost
Free

Directions
At the South Padre Island Convention Centre,
north of town.

What's Fun about South Padre Island?

VISITING MATAMOROS, MEXICO

One of South Padre Island's greatest assets

The narrated, guided bus tour begins at South Padre Island and takes you past the Port of Brownsville, the shrimp basin, through Brownsville, and across the Rio Grande to one of the finest border cities, Matamoros, Mexico (25 miles away on Texas Hwy 48).

The tour combines sightseeing of prominent historical sites, shopping in the Old and New Markets, and concludes with dining at Garcia's, a fine restaurant and curio shop, before heading back to South Padre Island.

Enjoy bargain shopping for leather goods, handicrafts, pottery, silver, woven rugs, watches, jewelry, hand-blown glass and more. English-speaking shopkeepers are friendly with visitors from across the border. Shops in the New Market accept US currency and credit cards.

Gray Line Tours
Sunchase Mall
956-761-4343

Original Tour Company
P.O. Box 2422
956-761-3139

Surftran Airport Shuttle and Tours
South Padre Island
956-761-1641 • 800-962-8497

Wanting to visit Matamoros on your own? There are two ways to access the city from Brownsville: the Gateway International Bridge and B & M Railroad Bridge (the old bridge). Both require a toll of $.25 to enter Mexico and $.35 to return. If you drive across, it costs $1.00 to go and $1.50 to return. (Be sure to check your insurance to see if you are covered.) Passports or identification aren't necessary.

Entering Matamoros, you will find transportation to the market area and other areas. You can travel either by taxis, the Maxi Taxi, or the "free" bus. If using a taxi, be prepared to negotiate a fare before you go. The Maxi Taxi, a small yellow bus, travels the city and costs $.35. Just ask the driver if he is going to the "Mercado" and he will let you know when to get off and give you directions. The "free" bus, provided by the merchants, goes to the market area.

WATCH FOR THESE ANNUAL EVENTS

CharroDays
Brownsville
(February)

A three-day international celebration with food, live concerts, contests, arts and crafts in Brownsville's Washington Park. A "Mr. Amigo" is chosen to represent friendship.

Sand Castle Days
South Padre Island
(October)

Amateurs and masters compete for big bucks in this two-day beach event. Spectators are welcome, see elaborate masterpieces created in a 16-hour time period.

Semana Santa—Holy Week
South Padre Island
(March or April)

Thousands of Mexicans celebrate their national Mexican holiday on South Padre Island. This week has a huge impact on the island's economy.

Spring Break
South Padre Island
(March)

The place for college students as thousands descend upon SPI for relaxation, music, entertainment, water sports, food, nightlife, and beach activities.

What's Fun about  *South Padre Island?*

Texas International Fishing Tournament
South Padre Island
(August)
956-943-TIFT

Texas' largest bay and deep-sea tournament when anglers from all over come to compete.

Windsurfing Blowout
South Padre Island
(May)
956-761-6433 • 800-767-2373

South Padre Island is now recognized as a top windsurfing destination in the continental US. Recreational wind surfers compete in a slalom and long-distance race on "The Flats," a shallow area of Laguna Madre north of the SPI Convention Centre. The public is welcome to watch from the water's edge.

What's Fun about South Padre Island?

WATERSPORT RENTALS
Renting almost every kind imaginable

If you love the water, check these places out. The list of watersports and activities are endless, offering windsurfing, surfing, water skiing, snorkeling, parasailing, banana boats, and scuba diving. Take a ride in a hydroplane.

Rent boogie boards, sail boats, paddleboats, catamarans, jet skis, waverunners, and more.

Many of the major hotels offer rental services' including the Radisson Resort, the Holiday Inn Sunspree, and the Sheraton Fiesta Beach Resort.

Rental services are located along either the bay side or gulf side of the island.

Listed are some of the outfits that rent watersport equipment. Some offer lessons as well. Parrot Eyes and the Water Toys are the largest.

Coconuts
2301 Laguna Blvd. • 956-761-4218

Louie's Backyard
2305 Laguna Blvd. • 956-761-6406

Parrot-Eye WaterSports
6101 Padre Blvd. • 956-761-7619

Sonny's Beach Service
Radisson • 956-761-5594
Sheraton Fiesta • 956-761-5556
Holiday Inn Sunspree • 956-761-7270

What's Fun about South Padre Island?

Tequila Sunset
200 W. Pike • 956-761-6198

The Wetspot
208 W. Corral • 956-761-1122

Wanna Wanna
5100 Gulf Blvd. • 956-761-7688

Water Toys
204 W. Palm • 956-761-5170

Windsurf the Boatyard
212 W. Dolphin • 956-761-5061

Windsurf, Inc.
224 W. Carolyn • 956-761-1434

What's Fun about South Padre Island?

WHAT'S KIDS' STUFF?

Fun activities for families with younger children

South Padre Island has plenty of activities for everyone including kids. Here are activities they're bound to enjoy.

Ben's Fun & Sun
6701 Padre Blvd.
956-761-5429
At the north end of Padre Blvd.
Offers go-carts and 4-wheelers for the beach.

The Gladys Porter Zoo
500 Ringgold Street
Brownsville, TX 78520
956-546-7187
956-546-2177 Recording

Features a children's zoo and nursery. Their petting zoo has Nigerian dwarf goats, miniature mules, domestic chickens, and more.

Jeremiah's
Hwy 100 and Gulf Point
956-761-2131

Has waterslides for big kids as well as tots. Also a video arcade.

Three Flags over Padre
1201 Padre Blvd.
956-761-1947

Across from Sunchase Mall. Features go-carts, miniature golf, spaceballs, a Ferris wheel, video arcades, and more.

Island Equestrian Center
Close to Andy Bowie Park
956-761-4677 • 800-761-4677
Any child six years and under can ride ponies out on the beach.

University of Texas at Brownsville
Located at the Old Coast Guard Station. Offers summer camps for kids.

Sea Turtle, Inc.
5805 Gulf Blvd.
956-761-2544
Shows featuring endangered and injured sea turtles that will delight all ages.

What's Fun about South Padre Island?

WHERE TO EAT?

The Ten Best Places to Eat on the Island

South Padre Island has so many great restaurants, it was difficult to limit the list to ten. For great food, you won't go wrong with any of these.

Amberjack's Bayside Bar and Grill
209 W. Amberjack Street
956-761-6500

Opens daily for lunch and dinner. Great seafood with a view of the bay and causeway. Enjoy the sunset. Live entertainment upstairs. Television for sports events.

Blackbeards' Restaurant
103 E. Saturn
956-761-2962

Seafood, steaks, hamburgers, sandwiches. Great for lunch or dinner. One of South Padre's favorite steak and fresh seafood restaurants. Open daily 11a.m. – 11p.m.

Blue Rays Diner
410 Padre Blvd.
956-761-RAYS

Claimed to be "the Island's version of a Hard Rock Cafe" by Texas Monthly. Has a 1950's atmosphere with great burgers, sandwiches, seafood, pasta dishes, fantastic desserts, and a soda fountain. Go here for shakes and ice cream. Try the fresh Red Snapper Veracruz Style with a tomato sauce or sauteed shrimp over pasta in a chipotle sauce. Open for lunch and dinner.

LaJaiba Seafood Restaurant & Lounge
2001 Padre Blvd.
956-761-9878

Closed on Mondays. Offers great seafood: fish, shrimp, oysters, king crab, clam chowder. Advertises itself as the "home of the freshest seafood on the island." Tuesday through Sunday 11:30am – 2:30pm and 5pm – 9pm.

Louie's Backyard
2305 Laguna Blvd.
956-761-6406

Fantastic prime rib seafood buffet. All-you-can-eat prime rib, baked ham, catfish, hash puppies, broiled fish in lemon butter sauce, garden vegetables, fresh salads, and more. Great children's menus. Offering dining and dancing by the bay with a great view. Popular with Spring Breakers.

Padre Island Brewing Company
3400 Padre Blvd.
956-761-9585

Micro brewery, offers hand-tossed pizza, sandwiches, seafood, steak, quail, burgers, and more. Second story deck to watch the sunsets. Closed on Monday. Tuesday and Thursday 11:30am – 11pm and Friday and Saturday 11:30am – 1am.

Palmetto Inn Restaurant
1817 Padre Blvd.
956-761-4325

One of the oldest restaurants on the island. Serving both fantastic seafood and Mexican food.

Rovan's Restaurant Bakery and BBQ
5300 Padre Blvd.
956-761-6972

Excellent breakfasts served all day, starting at 6am. Their specialty is home-style cooking. Fresh bread, donuts, cakes, and pies. Offers all-you-can-eat buffets. Monday is Italian. Wednesday is Mexican. Thursday is Mesquite BBQ. Friday is a Fish Fry. And Saturday they serve prime rib. Closed Tuesday.

Sea Ranch Restaurant
1 Padre Blvd.
956-1314

Ranked as a "Top 500 restaurant in the U.S.," Specializing in red snapper and tender steaks. Very popular and sometimes crowded. Offers daily lunch specials and waterfront dining.

The Pantry Grill Room
708 Padre Blvd.
956-761-9331

In Franke Plaza. Includes a gourmet shop and delicatessen with burgers, homemade soups, salads, sandwiches, imported cheeses, and more. And fine dining with seafood, steaks, lamb, quail, and more.

What's Fun about South Padre Island?

WHERE TO STAY?

The Ten Best Places to Stay on the Island

There are many wonderful accommodations and limiting this list to the ten best was difficult. Most people prefer staying in condominiums. Call the resorts to make a reservations or call one of these agencies. Island Reservations (800-926-6926), Service 24 (800-828-4287), Sunny Isles Rental Service (800-221-0169), or Padre Rentals (800-292-7518).

The island's hotels offer options such as in-room maid service and on-site restaurants. Listed here are the two best, the Radisson and the Sheraton.

Other types of lodging such as motels, RV parks, and camping are also listed.

Bahia Mar Resort and Conference Center

6300 Padre Blvd. (On the Gulf)
956-761-1343 • 800-997-2373

Stroll the "River Walk" to the beach, a 12-story unit with 1, 2, and 3 bedrooms, heated swimming pool, tennis courts, jacuzzi, restaurant, cable T.V., and laundry facilities.

Bridgepoint

334 Padre Blvd. (Condos on the Gulf)
800-221-1402

Considered a favorite. This is the tallest structure on the island and includes units with a full kitchen, a washer and dryer, balconies, and a spectacular view of the Gulf and Laguna Madre bay.

Brown Pelican Inn (Bed and Breakfast)

207 W. Aries
956-761-2722

Overlooks Laguna Madre. A two-story clapboard beach house with wrap-around porches and 8 rooms with antiques. The suite has a kitchen and formal living room, great for families with children 12 and over.

Edgewater

2216 Gulf Blvd. (Condos on the Gulf)
800-447-4753

Two and three bedroom condos with full kitchen facilities, pool, jacuzzi, tennis courts, and cable TV.

Franke Plaza

708 Padre Blvd. (Condos on the Gulf)
956-761-4208

Caters to families. Two, three, and four bedroom units with indoor pool, tennis, and health club.

Inverness Resort

5600 Gulf Blvd. (Condos on the Gulf)
956-761-7919

Caters to families with 1 and 2 bedroom units, pool jacuzzi, cable TV, and laundry facilities.

Radisson Resort

500 Padre Blvd. (On the Gulf)
956-761-6511 • 800-333-3333

One of the best full-service hotels on the island. Single and double rooms with pool, jacuzzi, cable T.V., restaurant, and tennis courts.

What's Fun about  *South Padre Island?*

Sheraton Fiesta Beach Resort
310 Padre Blvd. (On the Gulf)
956-761-6551 • 800-672-4747

Another of the best full-service hotels on the island with single and double rooms, pool, tennis courts, restaurant, jacuzzi, and cable T.V.

Sunchase Beachfront
1010 Padre Blvd. (On the Gulf)
956-761-1660 • 800-433-3702

Right on the beach with 1, 2, 3, and 4 bedroom units, full kitchen facilities, grills, patio or balcony.

The Padre Grand
2100 Gulf Blvd. (Condos on the Gulf)
956-761-4951

One and two bedroom units with full kitchen, washer and dryer, living area, balcony. Caters to families.

What's Fun about South Padre Island?

UNIQUE PLACES TO SHOP
South Padre Island has cute boutiques and unique shops

South Padre Island has no fancy factory outlet or large shopping malls, but you'll find shops and boutiques with handcrafted goods and fine appeal.

Sisters Trading Company
410 Padre Blvd.
956-761-2896

Barbara
2201 Padre Blvd.
956-761-9329

A swanky boutique featuring fine clothing and jewelry.

Cat House
3812 Padre Blvd.
956-761-CATS

This is a cat-lover's boutique with everything imaginable having to do with cats.

Little Bits of Texas
3812 Padre Blvd.
956-761-1844

Have a Texas theme in mind? You'll find wonderful items like jewelry, artifacts, western art, and sculptures from all over the state.

Island Traders Book Store & Coffe Pub
104 W. Pompano
956-761-7455

Find that special book for this great vacation. Offers regional and other books for tourists.

Port Isabel General Store
407 Maxan
956-943-2486

Across the street from the Lighthouse in Port Isabel. A fun, cute little shop you'll want to be sure to visit. Features lighthouse memorabilia.

Downtown Harlingen's Jackson Street District
956-427-8703

A historic business district with restored storefronts and street lamps. On Jackson Street between Commerce and 4th Street in downtown Harlingen. From Expressway 77/83, travel east on Tyler to 4th Street. Turn left and go three blocks to Jackson Street, then go left.

Sunchase Mall
1004 Padre Blvd.
956-761-7711

With a movie theater and two floors of shops, this is a good place to spend the afternoon, especially if the weather is unpleasant.

A

AAA Village Inn 135
Abner Jackson Archeological Dig Site 52
Absolutely Everything Under the Wave 169
Action Charters 71
Affordable Offshore Fishing 158
Air Tours of Galveston Island 12
Ala Cat Fishing Charters Offshore Fishing 158
Alice Municipal Golf Course 184
Alister Square Inn 167
Alta's Star Trek 197
Amaze 'N Galveston 23
Amberjack's Bayside Bar and Grill 265
American Diving 242, 243
American National Tower 13
Anchor Bed & Breakfast 79
Ancient Oaks Campground 139
Andy Bowie Park 236
Annual Deep Sea Roundup 164
Annual King Ranch Hand Breakfast 205
Annual South Texas Ranching Heritage Festival 203
Annual Stage Door Canteen 203
Annual Texas Jazz Festival 205
Anthony's by the Sea 136
Antiquing Area 213
Apfel Park 21
Aransas Area Bay Fishing 120
Aransas Bay 196
Aransas Lighthouse 146
Aransas National Wildlife Refuge 107
Aransas Princess Condominiums 166
Aransas Wildlife Refuge 130
Art Center for the Islands 147
Art Center of Corpus Christi 174
Art League, Brazosport 56
ArtWalks 14
Ashton Villa 18
Asian Cultures Museum & Educational Center 175
Austin, Stephen F. 74
Avalon Boat, Bed & Breakfast 212

B

B & M Railroad Bridge 258
Back 40 Restaurant 133
Baffin Bay 196
Bahia Mar Resort 268
Bahia Rica Adventures 120
Bahia Vista R.V. Park 137
Barbara 271
Barklett's Restaurant 100

Index

Barry Badders Guide Service 120
Battle of Iwo Jima Momument 230
Bay & Flats Fishing & Hunting Guides 120
Bay Breeze Bed and Breakfast 212
Bayfest & Folklife Celebration 205
Bayfront Beach Park 87
Bayfront Cottages 135
Bayfront R.V. Park 103
Bayside Drive auto tour 231
Beach Resort Rentals, Surfside Beach 80
Beach Walk Adventures 157
Beachfront Inn 42
Beacon Charter Service 158
Beacon R.V. Park 137
Bentsen R.G.V. State Park 239
Ben's Fun & Sun 263
Best Buddies 38
Best Western Beachfront Inn 42
Best Western Inn By The Sea 135
Best Western Motel, Lake Jackson 79
Best Western Ocean Villa 168
Beulah's 165
Big Bang Weekend 204
Big Tree Trailer Inn & Cottage 139
Bikini Rover Rentals 237
Bill Busters Sportfishing 158

Bird Island 89
Bird Watching Sites 108, 148, 238
Bishop's House 18
Bishop's Tree 124
Blackbeard's Restaurant 100, 265
Blucher Park 176
Blue Heron Inn 136
Blue Rays Diner 265
Bob Hall Pier 195, 198
Boca Chica Beach 252
Boca Chica Wetlands & Beaches 239
Bolivat Ferry 15
Bolivar Lighthouse 15
Bolivar Peninsula 73
Botanical Gardens 179, 206
Bravo Party Boats 71
Brazoria County Historical Museum 58
Brazoria County Museum 52
Brazoria National Wildlife Refuge 59
Brazos Bend State Park 54
Brazos Mall 81
Brazosport Center for the Arts and Sciences 56
Breakaway Cruises 243
Breakwater Jetty 195
Breakway Jetty 198
Bridgepoint 269
Brown Pelican Inn 269

Brownsville Convention & Visitors Bureau 221
Brownsville Fine Arts Museum 219
Brownsville Golf and Recreation Center 246
Brownsville Trolley Tour 223
Buccaneer Bay Resorts 115
Buccaneer Day and Rodeo 203
Buy the Seashell, Surfside 81

C

Café Michael Burger 40
Calhoun County Museum 90
Capt. Allen Sifford's "Fish On" 197
Capt. Carl Wentrcek Guide Service 197
Capt. Elliott's Fishing Boats 71
Capt. Joe Rhyne 98
Capt. John Howell 126
Capt. John "Red" Childers 98
Capt. Jon Fails 197
Capt. Kenneth Griffin 98
Capt. Lynn V. Smith 98
Capt. R.H. "Dick" Keitt 98
Capt. Robert E. "Bob" Dooley 98
Capt. Ron Elkins 98
Capt. Shelby Stocks 98
Capt. Ted's 125
Capt. Terry Panknin 197
Capt. Wallace Kelly 197
Captain Clark's Narrative Cruises 180, 197
Carolina Skiff 73
Cat House 271
Cayman House 136
Celebration of Whooping Cranes 163
Centennial House 181
Center Stage 56
Chandler House 133, 136
Chandler, Mrs. Billie Trimble 175
Chaparral Motel 102
Charlie's Guide Service 158
Charlie's Pasture 157
Charros Fiesta 259
Chocolate Bayou Park 87
Choke Canyon State Park 177
Christmas House 182
Christmas in the Park 74
Circle W. R.V. Park 137
City National Bank Building 19
Clark's Restaurant & Marina 100
Cline's Landing 166
Clute Municipal Park 75, 76
Coastal Studies Laboratory 241, 248
Coconuts 261
Cole Park 176, 206
Cole Park Pier 195, 198

Colonel Paddleboat 28
Columbia Lakes Resort and Conference Ctr 65
Confederate Air Force Museum 220
Connie Hagar Cottage Sanctuary 110
Copano Bay State Fishing Pier 108, 122
Copano Designs 127
Copeland's DBA (Adventurer) 158
Copeland's Marine 197
Coral Cay Condominiums 166
Corpus Christi Bay 196
Corpus Christi State University 176
Corpus Christi Greyhound Racing 183
Cottonwood Creek Golf Course 244
Crab-N Restaurant 133
Crabbing Sites 61, 111
Crazy Cajun 165
Crystal Blue Charters 158
Cygnet House 136

D

David Taylor Classic Car Museum 16
David's Charters 71
Davis Charters, Brazosport 71
Deep Sea Diving, Brazosport 62
Deep Sea Headquarters 150
Dellanera RV Park 45
Demonstration Bird Gardens & Wetland Pond 112
Dentoni's Pizza 207
DiBella's Italian Restaurant 39
Dickens On The Strand 36
Disc Golf, Clute 76
Discovery Channel Store 38
Discovery Pyramid 29
Dockside Restaurant and Patio 165
Dolphin Docks 150
Dolphin Watching on Laguna Madre bay 243
Don's Guide Service 198
Dow Chemical Texas Operations Tour 64
Dow, Willard 64
Downtown Harlingen's Jackson Street District 272
Dunes Condominiums 166

E

"E" Street Gallery 14
E.M.S. Chili Cook-Off 164
East Beach 21
Easy Going Charters 71
EconoLodge 42
Edgewater 269
El Constante Condominiums 211

El Patio Restaurant 100
Elissa 34, 35, 39
Elliott Guide Service 159
Enterprise Boutique 140
Estelle Stair Gallery & Studio 127
Executive Inn 102

F

Fennessey Ranch Wildlife Tours 109
Fiesta Air Show 220
Fiesta in La Playa 131
Fish Tales 40, 169
Fisherman's Wharf 34, 39, 150, 254
Fishin' Fever 159
Fishing Pier, The 255
Fishing Piers 32, 122
FKR Bed & Breakfast 212
Fly it Port "A" 169
For the Good Times II 63
Formosa Wetlands Walkway & Alcoa Birding Tower 88
Fort Brown Municipal Golf Course 246
Fort Velasco 72
Frame of Mine Gallery & Frame 127
Frames & Thangs 127
Franke Plaza 269
Fred Jones Nature Sanctuary 177

Freeport Municipal Golf Course 65
Freeport Municipal Park 54
Freespool and Ladyfish Charters 159
Friends of Connie Hagar 110
Fulton Fishing Pier 122
Fulton Mansion State Historical Park 113
Fulton Oysterfest 131
Fun Sports, South Padre 237

G

G & S Marine, Inc. 159
Gabe Lozano Sr. Golf Course 184
Gaido's 39
Gallery Row 14, 46
Galvan House 187
Galveston Area Map 8
Galveston Country Club 25
Galveston County Pocket Parks 21
Galveston Fishing Pier 32
Galveston Harbour Tours 17
Galveston Island Hilton Resort 43
Galveston Island Municipal 25
Galveston Island Railroad Museum 34
Galveston Island State Park 22, 45
Galveston Party Boats, Inc. 33
Galveston Historic Museum 19
Galvez 43

Gary Clouse Fishing & Hunting 120
Gary Osborne Fine Art 147
Gateway International Bridge 258
GCCA Take-A-Kid Tournament 163
Gladys Porter Zoo 224, 239, 263
Golfing, Brazosport 65
Golfing in the Rio GrandE Valley 244
Golfing on Galveston Island 25
Goose Island Oak 124
Goose Island State Park
    114, 124, 130, 138, 139
Goose Island State Park Fishing
    Pier 122
Gordon 69
Gordons's Restaurant 100
Grande-Grossman House 187
GrandView Restaurant and Bar 207
Gray Line Tours, Sun Chase Mall 257
Great Mosquito Festival 75
Great Storm Theater 11, 31, 34
Great Texas Birding Classic 204
Green Hornet Fishing Guide
    Service 120
Guadalupe Delta Wildlife
    Management Area 88
Gugenheim House 187
Gulf Stream Stables 37
Gulfstream Condominiums 211

H

Half Moon Reef Lighthouse 95
Hans A. Suter Wildlife Area 177
Hanson Riverside County Park 54
Happy Bottoms Charters 159
Harbor Inn Bayfront 210
Harbor Playhouse 186
Harlingen Country Club 245
Hatch Bend County Club 91
Hazel Bazemore County Park 176
Heritage Park 187
Heritage Trail Tour 221
High Island 73
Hilltop Community Center 177
Hilton Resort 43
Hogg, Gov. James 74
Holiday Inn Emerald Beach 209
Holiday Inn Express 135
Holiday Inn Express, Clute 79
Holiday Inn Gulf Beach Resort 210
Hook Guide Service 159
Hoopes' House 137
Horace Caldwell Pier 151
Hotel Blessing 101
Hotel Galvez 43
Hotel Lafitte 101
Howard Johnson Suites 42
Hummer/Bird Celebration 131

Hummingbird Lodge And Education Center 137
Hummingbird Studio 127
Hunt's Castle 135
Hydro Sport Scuba 63

I

IMAX Ridefilm Theater 29
IMAX Theater, Galveston 28
Indian Point 177, 195
Indian Point Pier 198
Indianola Beach 88
Indianola Beach Park 86
Indianola Town Site 96
Ingleside Navy Days 204
Ingram's Guide Service 198
Innuendo 14
International Kite Museum 188, 206
Inverness Resort 269
Investigator Fishing Charters 159
Ironhead Charter Service 159
Isla Blanca Park 241, 248
Island Equestrian Center 249, 264
Island House Condominiums 210
Island Reservations 268
Island RV Resort 168
Island Traders Book Store & Coffe Pub 272

J

J. Verschoyle Working Studio 128
Jackson, Abner 52
Jalufka House 187
Jeremiah's 263
Jesus Bautista Moroles Granite Studio 128
Jim's Pier 254
John F. Kennedy Causeway 176
Johnston's Sportfishing 71

K

Kemp's Ridley Sea Turtle Research Center 37, 251
Kids' Day at Executive Surf Club 206
Kiko's Mexican Food Restaurant 207
King Ranch 189
Kings Crossing Country Club 184
Kites Unlimited 38
Kitty's Purple Cow 78
Kolache Shop 78
Kontiki Beach Resort Motel 135
Kveton, Dave 71

L

L.E. Ramey Municipal Course 184
La Bahia 207
La Posada De Kingsville 205

La Quinta Galveston 43
La Quinta Inn, Clute 80
Lagoons R.V. Park 138
Laguna Atascosa National Wildlife Refuge 231, 238
Laguna Madre Nature Trail 238, 250
Laguna Reef Hotel/Suites 136
Laguna Salada Safaris 120
LaJaiba Seafood Restaurant & Lounge 266
Lake Corpus Christi State Recreation Area 178
Lake Jackson Historical Museum 52
Lake Jackson Wilderness Park 54
Lamar Cemetery 116
Lamar Oak 124
Landry's Seafood House 41, 207
LaSalle Monument 96
LaSalle's Cross 96
Lichtenstein House 187
Lighthouse Beach & Bird Sanctuary R.V. Park 103
Lighthouse Beach Park 86
Lighthouse Restaurant and Catering Company 208
Little Bits of Texas 271
Little Gallery 127
Littles-Martin House 187
Live Oak Country Club 115
Living in the Stars Exhibit 29
Lone Angler Guide Service 120
Lone Star Flight Museum 27
Longhorn Steak and Ale 208
Louie's Backyard 261, 266
Luther Hotel 101

M

Mad Island Marsh Preserve 89
Magnolia Beach Park 86, 88
Mamma Mia's 208
Mardi Gras 36
Marina Grand Hotel 209
Mark Williams Guide Service 121
Marshall's Guide Service 159
Matagorda Island 89
Matagorda Island Lighthouse 96
Matagorda Island State Park 92
Mayan Princess Condominiums 166
McCampbell House 187
Mercado Express 257
Merriman Bobys House 187
Mexican Café 40
Migration Celebration 53, 75
Mike Sydows Fishing & Hunting 121
Mini Golf Course 23
Moody Gardens 28

Moody Mansion 18
Moonlight Bay Bed & Breakfast 101
Moore Plaza 213
Mosquito Festival 75
Museum, Elissa 35
Museum, Galveston 19
Museum, Galveston Railroad 24
Museum of Natural Science, Brazosport 57
Museum, Texas Seaport 35
Mustang Island Stables 153
Mustang Island State Park 152, 168
MV Wharf Cat 126

N

Nate's Steakhouse & Seafood 41
National Audubon Society 227
Nature Center and Planetarium, Brazosport 57
Nature Conservancy of Texas 89
Naval Station Ingleside 192
Neale House 219
Nesloney Fishing & Hunting 121
Niche Gallery 128
Norman Spears Guide Service 121
North Shore Country Club 185
Nueces Bay Pier 195, 198
Nueces County Pier 151
Nueces River Park 178

O

Ocean Hideaway R.V. Park 138
Ocean Quest Dive Center 242
Ocean Star Offshore Energy Ctr 30
Old River Trading Co., Freeport 81
Old Three Hundred 74
Omni Bayfront Hotel 209
Omni Marina Hotel 209
On the River Restaurant 78
Opera House 26
Original Mexican Café 40
Original Tour Company 257
Oso Beach Golf Course 185
Oso Pier 195, 198
Outboard Fishing Tournament 164

P

Packery Channel County Park 178
Paddleboat, The Colnel 28
Padre Activity Rentals 237
Padre Grand 270
Padre Island Brewing Company 266
Padre Island National Seashore 178, 193
Padre Rentals 268
Padre Staples Mall 213

Palacios Golf Course 91
Palm Beach 22, 28
Palmetto Inn Restaurant 267
Palmito Ranch Battlefield 226
Palo Alto Battlefield National Historic Site 225
Pantry Grill Room 267
Parrot-Eye WaterSports 261
Pelican Island 32
Pelican's Landing Restaurant 165
Peregrine Gallery 128
Pharaoh Country Club 185
Phoenix Bakery and Coffee House 41
Pier 21 46
Pioneer R.V. Park 168
Point Comfort Park 87
Point Wildlife Management Recreation Area 55
Poretto Beach 22
Port A, U.S.A. Shops 169
Port Aransas Birding Center 148
Port Aransas Community Theater 154
Port Aransas Wetlands Park 149
Port Aransas Wild Game and Seafood Dinner 163
Port Bolivar Lighthouse 15
Port Isabel General Store 272
Port Isabel Historical Museum 234
Port Isabel Lighthouse State Historical Park 235
Port Lavaca State Fishing Pier 94
Port Motel 102
Port of Freeport 67
Port Royal Ocean Resort 167
Port Royal Ocean Resort Condominiums 211
Potato Patch 77
Powderhorn Lake Area 88
Powderhorn R.V. Park 103
Powhatau House 18
Princess 63
Private Deep Sea Charters 159

Q

Queen Isabella Causeway 235
Queen's Line, Inc. 160
Quintana Beach County Park 80
Quintana County Park Fishing Pier 71
Quintana Island Bird Sanctuary 55

R

R & R Charter Service 254
R.A. Apfel Park 21
Radisson Resort 270
Railroad Depot, Southern Pacific 222
Railroad Museum 24, 34

Rainforest Pyramid 28
Ramada Inn Bayfront 210
Ramada Inn Resort 43
Rancho Viejo Country Club 247
Ranger Cemetery 95
Red drum production 69
Red Snapper Inn 77
Republic of Texas Bar and Grill 208
Ridefilm Theater 29
Ridley Sea Turtle Research Center 37
Rio GrandE Valley Historical Museum & Complex 232
Rob and Bessie Welder Wildlife Refuge 178
Rockport Art Festival 132
Rockport Artists' Gallery 128
Rockport Beach Park 117, 130
Rockport Center for the Arts 118, 128, 130
Rockport Center for the Arts Gift Shop 140
Rockport Country Club 115
Rockport Seafair 132
Rovan's Restaurant Bakery and BBQ 267

S

Sabal Palm Audubon Center and Sanctuary 227, 239
Sailsman Charter Boat Services 160
Samuel May Williams Home 18
San Bernard National Wildlife Refuge 68, 73
San Jose Island and North Jetty 151, 157
San Jose Island Jetty Boat 156
San Luis Pass County Park 55, 80
San Luis Pass Fishing Pier 71
San Luis Resort and Conference Center 44
Sand Castle Days 259
Sandcastle Condominiums 167
Sandollar Pavilion Restaurant 134
Santa Anna National Wildlife Refuge 228, 240
Sea Center Texas 69, 73
Sea Pals, Surfside 81
Sea Ranch Fishing Pier 254, 255
Sea Ranch Restaurant 248, 267
Sea Sands Condominiums 167
Sea Searchers II 63
Sea Turtle, Inc. 251, 264
Sea Turtle Research Center 37
Seadrift Bayfront Park 86

Seaport Museum 35
Seawall 20
Seawolf Park 32
See-wall Mural 20
Semana Santa—Holy Week 259
Serendipity Resort 103
Shady Oaks R.V. Park 138
Shallow Water Charters 160
Shallow Water Roundup and Seafood Bash 164
Shelling Sites 70, 157, 252
Shells and Souvenirs 38
Sheraton Fiesta Beach Resort 270
Sidbury House 187
Silver Fox Trading Company 169
Simon Michael School and Gallery of Fine Art 129
Sinton Municipal Golf Course 185
Sisters of Schoenstatt Convent and Shrine 119
Sisters Trading Company 271
Sleepy Hollow R.V. Park 138
Sonny's Beach Service 261
South Jetty 151
South of Reason Charters 160
South Padre Island Convention Center 250
South Padre Island Golf Club 247
South Texas Institute for the Arts 194
South Texas Ranching Heritage Festival 203
Southern Pacific Railroad Depo 222
Sport fishing 32, 71, 97
Sportsplex Marina 150
Spring Break 259
Stars & Stripes 204
Station Street Pier 151
Stella Maris Chapel 116
Steve Russell Gallery 127
Stewart Beach 23
Stillman House 223, 229
Strand 10, 34, 36, 46
Sun Island 89
Sunchase Beachfront 270
Sunchase Mall 272
Sunny Isles Rental Service 268
Sunrise Mall 213
Sunset Sounds 154
Surfside Grill & Pizza 77
Surfside Historical Museum 72
Surfside Motel, Surfside Beach 80
Surfside Waterslides 76
Surftran Airport Shuttle and Tours 258
Symphony Orchestra, Brazosport 57

T

T-Heads 176
Tarpon Inn 167
Tecolote Charter Service 121
TejanoFest 204
Tejas Gallery and Gifts 129
Tequila Sunset 262
Texas Air Museum 233
Texas International Fishing
    Tournament 260
Texas Maritime Museum 123, 130
Texas nature Adventure 73
Texas Seaport Museum 35
Texas Sport Fishing & Yacht Sales 71
Texas State Aquarium 199, 206
The Bar-B-Q Man Restaurant 208
The Big Fisherman 134
The Big Tree 124
The Blue Ghost 201
The Boiling Pot 134
The Habitat 137
The Old Peanut Butter Warehouse 46
The Original Mexican Café 40
The Wetspot 262
The Wharf Cat 162
Third Coast Adventures Guide
    Service 121
Three Flags over Padre 263
Tightline Fishing Charters 121
Tony Country Club 245
Trailer Inn By The Bay 138
Train Museum, Brazoria 76
Treasure Hills Country Club 246
Tremont House 44
Trout Street Bar and Grill 165
Turtle, Kemp's Ridley Sea 251
Turtle Research Center 37

U

Uncle Buggies, South Padre 237
University of Texas at Brownsville 264
University of Texas Marine Science
    Institute 161
Upper Laguna Madre 196

V

Valonari's Restaurant 134
Valley Inn & Country Club 244
Valley Nature Center 240
Varner, Martin 74
Varner-Hogg Plantation State Historical
    Park 55, 74
Victorian Bed and Breakfast 44

W

Wanna Wanna 262

Water Coaster and Patio Bar 23
Water Street Market 213
Water Toys 262
Wateredge R.V. Park 138
Waterfront Art Market 202
WaterStreet Seafood Co. 208
Waterworld Charters 160
Whaling Wall 250, 256
Whispering Winds Golf & Learning
    Center 245
Whooping Crane Tours 125, 162
William Neale House 219
Williams Home 18
Williams Party Boats 33
Willie Manchew 75
Windsurf the Boatyard 262
Windsurfing Blowout 260
Windway Studio-Gallery 129
Woody Acres Trailer Park 139
Woody's Sport Center 150
World of Discovery 200, 206

Y

Yamato 40